AF335058

Gallery Books
Editor: Peter Fallon

DONE INTO ENGLISH

Pearse Hutchinson

DONE INTO ENGLISH

Collected Translations

Gallery Books

Done into English
is first published
simultaneously in paperback
and in a clothbound edition
on 27 November 2003.

The Gallery Press
Loughcrew
Oldcastle
County Meath
Ireland

ISBN 1 85235 315 5 (*paperback*)
     1 85235 316 3 (*clothbound*)

A CIP catalogue record for this book
is available from the British Library.

The Gallery Press acknowledges the financial assistance
of An Chomhairle Ealaíon / The Arts Council, Ireland.

Contents

© Xosé Vizoso

Introduction

From the Christian Brothers in Synge Street we learned English, Irish, and Latin (to put them in purely alphabetical order). Until the age of fifteen there was nothing I loved better than studying, especially those three languages.

After school, I kept up English — it's compulsory. Irish I half let go for a few years. Latin I just let go, much to my present regret. But I suppose enough of it must already have sunk in to be of help to me when I came to grips with modern languages derived from it.

When I was twenty-one my mother and Father Senan OFM Cap, that unrivalled Maecenas of the 1940s and '50s, ganged up on me to force me into an Arts course at UCD. I never wanted to go to that or any other university, but it was a meal-ticket, thanks to Senan, that Ciarraíoch beannaithe, who actually believed that poets had a right to eat, even young poets who drank too much, or wanted to (he ate too much).

I stuck it for a year-and-a-half, then got out. But at least in that time I'd got well into Spanish, and fallen in love with it, and also learnt a fair bit of Italian. Spanish (or rather Castilian: the dominant language of the Spanish state) seemed to me at first a 'stronger' sounding language than Italian — until I heard a lecturer called Signora Gaidoni reciting D'Annunzio's poem 'Le Onde' (The Waves). A fine poet and a fine interpreter can bring out, in a language, unexpected strengths, and, if need be, hidden softnesses — music, of different kinds — glories that do not *always* leap to the ear in the daily street. As I rediscovered a few years later when the Dutch poet Adriaan Morriën read me some of his poems.

After my mother died in 1968, I found among her papers a postcard I'd sent her from her siblings' home in Uddingston when I was seven, saying: 'When I grow up I'll take you to sunny Spain.' Where I got that idea from, God only knows. Nothing ever came of it.

Of more consequence, perhaps, is the fact that towards the end of the Spanish Civil War, in other words when I was eleven or twelve, my father took me to a meeting in the Round Room of the

Introduction

Mansion House, which was addressed by a Basque priest called Father Laborda. I remember little of it, except that this man of God made an impassioned speech in defence of the Spanish Republic which, when I looked back on it a few years later, was quite an eye-opener, given that the people of Saorstát Éireann were massively, though not with entire success, bamboozled into imagining that God was on the side of the anti-Republican insurgent Franco.

In 1950, aged twenty-three, I went on holiday to Portugal and Spain with a Trinidadian friend. We boarded the *Highland Mail* at Tilbury. On reaching Vigo, passengers were allowed on shore for four hours. That was my first time on Spanish soil. That it was, in greater truth, Galician soil, was not then apparent to me.

That night the upper deck was taken over by scores — it seemed hundreds — of Galician emigrants on their way to Buenos Aires or Montevideo. It was like an American wake. It *was* an American wake. And the music was definitely not flamenco. Some of it sounded almost Irish, some of it almost Breton. So I began to sense, dimly at first, that the Madrid/Castilian/centralist slogan, 'España no es más que una' (Spain is One and only One), mightn't be altogether true.

After two days in Lisbon we got to Andalusia: the Promised Land. Heat, light, sensuality. Machado and Unamuno remained my favourites, but this was the native land of Lorca, of Prados, even of that by no means always stern poet, Cernuda. His poem 'An Idle Man' (page 110) and Prados's 'Sleeping on the Grass' (page 107) are still, for me, magnificent assertions, against the lethal perversion of work enshrined in the 'work-ethic' (more properly called the overwork-ethic), of the right to leisure, even to laze.

An early poem by Cernuda is called 'Andaluz' (Andalusian). In it he says that name is the most beautiful of all words. Now if you break that word up, into 'Anda, luz', it means: 'Walk, light'. That early September of 1950, in Seville, in Granada, in Córdoba, the light walked for me as it never had before, and I walked through the light I'd always longed for.

But as we sat, Bert Achong from Port-o'-Spain and I, in solitary splendour at a sidewalk table in the Parque Maria Luisa in Seville, basking in early-September heat and light and wolfing down cray-fish, a raggy boy of about ten came up to us and thrust the stump of his left arm right in our faces.

The following year I left Ireland on All Fools' Day, 'determined' to live in Spain 'for ever'. Alone this time, I took the same boat, from Tilbury to Lisbon by way of Vigo. Once again the *rias* of Vigo were breathtakingly beautiful, surpassing even Dublin Bay. Once again the Galician emigrants boarded the boat at Vigo, and once again their American wake went on into the small hours.

Browsing in a Lisbon bookshop, I came across the *Cantigas d'Amigo*, the amorous song-poems by the Galician and Portuguese troubadours of the 13th and 14th centuries. These brief lyrics, based on parallelism and repetition, had a freshness and immediacy far removed from the densely wrought elabora-tions of the old Provençal masters. They came singing and lively across the centuries, complete news to me, one of the loveliest revelations of my whole life.

They must have been a lovely revelation to Ernesto Monaci too, when he first found them in the *Vatican Songbook*. That great collection, consisting of more than 1200 Galician and Portuguese lyrics, was virtually forgotten, or known in fragments only, until 1875, when Monaci published 'Il canzoniere portoghese della Bibliotecha Vaticana' in Halle.

The book I bought in Lisbon was a Portuguese selection, edited by Costa Pimpão. It travelled with me round Europe, then vanished into thin air. But before that I'd sung songs from it on deserted roads in Portugal, Andalusia, the Suisse Romande and Austria, and broadcast versions of them on the old BBC Third Programme. The magnificent producer was David Thomson, but a colleague of his took me to task for overdoing the Portuguese aspect at the expense of the Galician. I now think he was right. So, partly because in many cases nobody seems to know for sure exactly where many of the troubadours came from, and partly for the sake of consistency, I've erred here, as far as the spelling of the names go, on the side of Galician.

I tried to get work in Madrid, but couldn't. So I went to Geneva where friends got me a job with the International Labour Office, translating from French and Spanish. (When and how I learnt French I've no idea.)

Among my colleagues at the ILO was a group of Spanish Republican exiles. They sometimes invited me to eat paella with them. One was Catalan. He was remarkably taciturn. An English colleague, who loved Spain, told me Catalans were 'not really Spanish'. I was puzzled.

There was nothing at all puzzling, though, about the bitterness those Republican refugees felt about the Allies' failure, or refusal, to move against the Fascist dictator Franco once they'd put paid to Hitler and Mussolini. The war *had* been fought in defence of democracy, hadn't it? And Franco and his bully-boys were Fascists, weren't they? Not at all: they were bulwarks of the Christian West against Communism. That must surely count as one of the worst betrayals of the twentieth century.

From Geneva I took a couple of months out to attend the Salzburg Seminar in American Studies. There I got to know Huyck van Leeuwen, co-editor of the literary magazine *Libertinage*, who invited me to Holland. Before going there I started to learn Dutch.

National stereotypes are unfailingly dismal. For example: the despicable gibe in *The Third Man* about the Swiss and cuckoo-clocks. The Dutch are too often regarded as dull. Unpoetic. But in the primer I studied there was a short selection of Dutch sayings. One leapt from the page: 'Uilen naar Athene dragen.' Literally, to bring owls to Athena. In other words, to carry coals to Newcastle. Fine poetry has been made out of miners' battles; but the Dutch version of that universal thought is a poem in itself. (The Galician version, by the way, is equally rich: 'Levar auga ó mar' — To bring water to the sea.)

When I came back to Dublin in late 1953, I brought with me about a dozen books in Dutch, mainly verse. But reading or re-reading twelve books isn't enough for very long. So I went to the Dutch embassy in Fitzwilliam Square and asked to see the Cultural Attaché. There wasn't one. But finally a large fierce Dutch woman came out to the hall and lent an impatient ear. I told her I wanted to go on reading Dutch, not to lose it. I was hoping the embassy might be able to lend me some books, or put me in touch with someone in the Dutch community who could.

She glared at me in disbelief. 'All the Dutch people here are business-folk,' she said. 'And anyway, nobody reads Dutch.' That wouldn't happen now, I'm glad to say. But I couldn't help, at that brutal moment, thinking of my friends in Holland, who not only read Dutch but wrote in it. I thought of their kindness and hospitality, and of the warm inscriptions they'd written in the books of theirs they'd given me, and I nearly blurted all that out to that woman; but I thought better of it just in time, preferring not to insult them by mentioning them to the likes of her.

Dutch and Flemish are, basically, the same language, Flemish being the Dutch of Belgium. Of the four poets in the Dutch/Flemish section, Hendrik Marsman and Judith Herzberg belong to Holland, Paul van Ostaijen and Joris Iven to Belgium.

In September 1954 I went to Barcelona with a girl called Sammy Sheridan. We knew we could get work there teaching English, our intention being to spend the winter there and leave for Andalusia in the spring. But we fell in love with Barcelona, which, despite the tyranny of Franco and the poverty, was still — not already, but still — an exciting city to live in, especially perhaps if you were young and foreign and had as little as possible to do with the police. So we never did get to Andalusia, except for six magnificent weeks in Pedregalejos, near Málaga, one summer.

Three of our young students invited us out on the town one night. We all had a great time. Halfway through the festivities I noticed that every now and then these young men couldn't help speaking Catalan to each other for a sentence or two, instead of the Spanish (Castilian) they'd been courteously speaking to us all evening.

I could understand about a third of what they were saying in Catalan. It was tantalizing. So after a couple more occasions like that I was already thinking of learning Catalan (it was, after all, being spoken all around me), when a schoolteacher who sometimes shared our table in the restaurant called Culleretes, in the Calle Quintana, near the Ramblas, showed us, over the coffee, a book of poems in Catalan. Our fellow-diner's name was Josep Maria Bordas (he later translated Quasimodo into Catalan). The poet's name was Salvador Espriu. Bordas translated one of the poems into Castilian for us ('El Ninot' — The Puppet, or Manikin), then read it to us in the original. If ever I felt what Edmund Wilson called 'the shock of recognition', that was it.

In those days there wasn't a single book in Catalan to be seen in the bookshop windows of Barcelona, or inside on the shelves either. Except, if you were lucky, tucked away in a cranny of some small secondhand bookshop down a sidestreet. A friendly acquaintance contrived to get hold of a Catalan grammar for me, published in the early days of the Republic.

After a while I started translating, the first poem being, naturally, Espriu's 'Manikin'. It's not in this book, having long since vanished into thin air, perhaps from the top of that suicide's paradise, the Expiatory Temple of the Sagrada Familia (only *one* of Gaudí's masterpieces) — or under a raucous old tram, like Gaudí himself.

When Franco's forces defeated the Republic, and with it Catalan autonomy, the Catalan language was banned, except in private. As David H Rosenthal wrote in the foreword to his translation of Mercè Rodoreda's great Civil War novel *La Plaça del Diamant* (*The Time of the Doves*, Arena, 1986):

> *'Catalan books were burned, Catalan newspapers suppressed, and offices were hung with signs saying "No ladres, habla el idioma del Imperio Español."'* (Don't bark, speak the language of the Spanish Empire.)

I got to know Espriu and other Catalan poets such as Carles Riba (who'd spent part of his exile in Dublin) and started translating them. Then, when John Jordan came out to spend Christmas with Sammy and me, he introduced us to the young English poet, PJ Kavanagh, whom he'd known at Oxford. Patrick was working for the British Institute. We quickly became good friends, and he soon set about persuading the Institute to put on a reading of Catalan verse.

The authorities, somewhat to my surprise, granted the Institute permission for this, and on the 7th of June, 1955, Espriu, Riba, Joaquim Horta, Blai Bonet and Marià Manent read their poems in Catalan to a packed audience, and I read my translations.

In 1957 I came back to Ireland, but returned to Barcelona in 1961, with a friend called Ernie Hughes. Soon after arriving I met for the first time the poet Pere Quart, whose books *Terra de naufragis* (*Land of Shipwrecks*, 1956) and *Vacances pagades* (*Holidays with Pay*, 1960) had by then become a rallying point for young Catalan poets and rebels.

Kavanagh was no longer in Barcelona. His place in the Institute had been taken by an amiable young man called John Whybrow, who arranged another bilingual reading on the 15th of March, 1962. Among those taking part were Espriu, again, and for the first time Pere Quart and Francesc Vallverdú.

The Institute was in the spacious boulevard known as the Diagonal. I met Pere Quart in a bar not far from there, and we walked to the Institute together. This white-bearded man was well over six foot. When we got to the door of the Institute he stopped, looked down at me, took my hand in his, and said: 'I want you to know how much this means to us.'

In 1961 the poet Marià Manent asked me to translate into English thirty poems by his old friend Josep Carner, long an exile in Brussels. Manent and other friends of Carner's were hoping to get the Nobel Prize for him. That would make it easier for him to return to his native Catalonia, despite 'the language of Empire'. Manent gave me a loan of Carner's collected poems, allowing me to choose which thirty. And he paid me handsomely.

That bilingual book was published in 1962 by Dolphin Books of Oxford (run by another exile, Joan Gili). Carner did not win the Nobel Prize, but he did return, for a while, to his native place, in 1970.

Espriu's seventyfour-poem sequence, *La pell de brau* (*The Bull-skin*) was published in 1960. I think it was three years later that a wealthy admirer of Espriu commissioned me to translate it into English. She too paid me handsomely. When it was done, negotiations began between a Dublin publisher (no longer with us) and a Barcelona publisher, with a view to joint publication. Why that fell through, I've no idea.

'The bull-skin' is an old Jewish name for Spain. In the perceptive introduction to Espriu's *Selected Poems* (Carcanet, 1997), the translator, Louis J Rodrigues, mentions the poet's 'obsessive interest in Jewish mysticism' and claims that 'if there is any single predominant influence to be observed in Espriu's writings . . . it is that of the Bible — the Books of Job, Ecclesiastes, and Psalms in the Old Testament, and the Acts of the Apostles in the New, being the most significant'.

I've chosen twenty-three of my versions from *The Bull-skin* to publish here. In his prologue to the second edition of the bilingual (Catalan/Castilian) version of *La pell de brau*, which I believe to be one of the greatest works of the twentieth century, Espriu refers to his masterpiece as 'how a man from the Iberian periphery tried, some time ago, to understand the complex peninsular enigma'.

And these four lines from the work itself (see section 6, page 159) go straight to the heart of the matter:

> *at the heart of envy we saw with dread*
> *the great crime of Sepharad take root:*
> *the sin so unendingly sad*
> *of triumphless war between brothers.*

Basque and Galician suffered equally with Catalan under Franco's long tyranny. We all need a second life — a second chance, that is — and if I was granted that, by which time the Basques might be independent (and Ireland united), I'd be sure to learn Basque early on. It's a bit late now.

With Franco in power Galician disappeared from the schools and from public life in general. You could lose your job for speaking Galician. Or be clapped in jail. A pro-Franco leaflet circulating in Galicia in 1942 hectored: 'Be a patriot. Not a barbarian. If you are a proper gentleman you must speak our official language, that is: Castilian. Long live Spain and Discipline and the Language of Cervantes. Up Spain!'

In the '60s, as in Catalonia, a certain thaw set in. In 1962, Celso Emilio Ferreiro's book *Longa noite de pedra* (*Long Night of Stone*) appeared, and immediately became — like Pere Quart's books in Catalonia — a rallying point for Galician poets and rebels. Eleven poems from that book are in this one.

In the nineteenth century the Galicians, like the Catalans and other subject peoples in many parts of Europe, had a great national re-awakening. Three Galician poets above all were emblematic of this: Eduardo Pondal, Manuel Curros Enríquez, and Rosalía de Castro. Rosalía's poem 'Castellanos de Castilla' (Castilians of Castile, page 45) is a masterpiece of invective, worthy of the great Scots Gaelic women poets of earlier centuries. If the bitterness in it — the hatred — is sometimes withering, it's worth remembering that such hate is most often born of hurt, of hurt love, of long deep hurt. The long night of stone stretches back long before Franco.

Sometime in the early '70s, in Bristol where he worked, inspired, and died, my great friend Toni Turull — Catalan poet, novelist, and critic — lent me the Galician number (July/October 1967) of a poetry magazine called *Claraboya* (*Skylight*), published in León. There I read for the first time Arcadio López-Casanova, Uxío Novoneyra, and Xosé-Luis Méndez Ferrín, among others. One of the two Novoneyra poems I liked best in that issue ('*O Moucho*' — *The Owl*), one of the finest lyric poems I've ever read, is to be found here (page 60). The other I translated into Irish, finding it went better into that language. But here, now, are the last three lines:

> *GALICIA, will my generation be the one to save you?*
> *Shall I walk one day from Caurel to Compostela through*
> *   liberated lands?*
> *No, it can't be in vain, this strength of our love!*

Since the transition to democracy after Franco's death in 1975, 'autonomous' governments have been set up in the Basque Country, Catalonia, and Galicia. The autonomous powers are far from adequate, but there is far more freedom to publish, at least in the case of Catalan and Galician. The present right-wing government in Madrid, led by Aznar, is, to put it mildly, less than sympathetic to the different identities of those three other nations, but despite the powerful begrudgers poetry is thriving.

The first poem I ever translated, when I was about nineteen, was from French: 'Mers-el-Kabir' by Valéry Larbaud. That too has vanished into thin air. The maxims and reflections of Vauvenargues have kept me company for twenty years. Not that I always agree with him. Voltaire admired and encouraged him and, later, Baudelaire came to love him. I couldn't resist turning one of this charming man's perceptive thoughts into verse.

Jean-Joseph Rabéarivelo of Madagascar (1901-1937) wrote in Malgache and Spanish as well as French. Those in the know say that French ideas crop up in his Malgache writings and Malgache visions in his French. And why not?

I'd like to have lived in Italy but never did. The longest I ever spent there was two months. I kept up with the language in a purely sporadic way until, many years ago now, I got to know Melita Cataldi of Turin — translator into Italian of the *Táin* and many other Irish works — and her husband Piero de Gennaro, and later, through Melita, Rosangela Barone, then director of the Italian Institute in Dublin, and translator of Caitlín Maude into Italian.

Knowing these generous, inspiring people gave me a new impetus to read Italian. And one of the books Piero and Melita brought me was *Le parole di legno — Poesia in dialetto del '900 italiano* (*Timberwords — 20th-Century Italian Dialect Poetry*), edited by Mario Chiesa and Giovanni Tesio, and published by Mondadori in 1984.

Many people in Piedmont, Milan, Friuli and Sardinia would dispute the term 'dialect'. Whatever about that, this two-volume anthology was a revelation to me. Poetry has been written for centuries, all over Italy, in the regional *parlate* (or *caint na ndaoine*). But after the Second World War there was a tremendous upsurge of modern poetry in these tongues, the two main inspirational forces being Pier Paolo Pasolini, whose first book was in Friulano (Furlan), and Tonino Guerra, who writes in Romagnolo.

Not that there weren't precursors — the Venetian Giacoma Noventa (1898-1960), for example. One of his best-known poems, 'Parché scrivo in dialeto?' (Why do I write in dialect?) goes like this:

> *Why do I write in dialect?*
> *Dante, Petrarch and him of the Ten Days,*
> *They wrote in Tuscan.*
> *I just follow their example.*

('Him of the Ten Days' means Boccaccio.)

I should, I suppose, point out, in a possibly vain attempt to stave off attack, that the few translations I've done from these non-standard, non-official Italian tongues have all been done with the help of cribs in that official language. This runs counter to translation principles I've proclaimed in the past, but (as in the case of some, by Pasolini and others, that I've done into Irish) I liked them too much to resist.

Why so few poems here from Irish? Well — hasn't the market been a bit overcrowded? Besides, I felt in a way that writing *in* Irish, as I still do, was enough. Maybe that's wrong. Maybe I'll do some more sometime . . .

A couple of final words: every poem in this book has been translated because I liked it, and that applies just as much to the two Catalan commissions.

Pearse Hutchinson

Pero Meogo

'I lay deep in the grass gazing . . .'

I lay deep in the grass gazing
    at the herd of deer grazing,
      my friend.

I watched in the green countryside
    the stags passing in their pride,
      my friend.

Then in the river I washed my clothes
    in homage to the gentle does,
      my friend.

And to show the bucks esteem
    I washed my hair in the gentle stream,
      my friend.

And when I'd washed and dried
    I bound my hair with pride,
      my friend.

In cloth of gold I bound it,
    I coiled the sun around it,
      my friend.

In gold I bound my hair
    and waited for you there,
      my friend.

I used to bind it so,
    waiting there for you,
      my friend.

PERO MEOGO

'Tell me, my daughter, so lovely and bold . . .'

Tell me, my daughter, so lovely and bold,
what kept you so long at the fountain so cold?
        (I'm in love.)

You never took longer, my daughter, to bring
your pitcher back full from the cold mountain spring!
        (I'm in love.)

I waited to watch, by the cold of the fountain,
the stags and the hinds coming down from the mountain.

I waited to watch, by the fountain's cool gleam,
the stags of the mountain return to the stream.

You're lying for love now, you're lying, my daughter:
there was never yet stag that returned to the water.
        (I'm in love.)

PERO MEOGO

'I want to know now, Mother...'

I want to know now, Mother,
so truthfully reply:
      dare my friend and lover
      address me when you're nigh?

I've just received a letter
from him, and would reply;
      but dare my friend and lover
      address me when you're nigh?

I'm off to the fountain, Mother,
to watch the drinking deer;
      but dare my friend and lover
      address me when you're near?

PERO VIVIÁEZ

'Because our mothers go to Simon's shrine . . .'

Because our mothers go to Simon's shrine
in Val de Prados, there to light the wick,
we, the young girls, are forced to walk
with our mothers to the holy shrine,
    where they burn candles, for themselves and us,
    and we, the young girls, dance there.

Our friends and lovers all assemble there
to see us, and we move before them
dancing with our bodies' glory;
and our mothers, all assembled there,
    burn candles, for themselves and us,
    and we, the young girls, dance there.

Our friends and lovers go to watch us
as we go dancing, and they can look
at girls that dance well, and have good looks;
and our mothers, because they want to,
    burn candles, for themselves and us,
    and we, the young girls, dance there.

Martín de Ginzo

'That beautiful creature commanded . . .'

That beautiful creature commanded
the tambourine be sounded.
    Girl, you're the picture of health,
    I'm dying of love.

That ripe and rosy queen
insisted on the tambourine.
    Girl, you're the picture of health,
    I'm dying of love.

She summoned the tambourine-player,
but little pleasure it gave her.
    Girl, you're the picture of health,
    I'm dying of love.

The tambourine-player did his best,
but his music brought her spirit no rest.

Johan Zorro

'I watched from the bank . . .'

I watched from the bank
the oarsmen embark.
  How pleasant it is on the riverbank.

I watched from on high
the oars being plied.
  How pleasant it is by the riverside.

I saw the men rowing,
and knew my love was going.
  How pleasant it is on the riverbank.

I saw the men departing,
and among them my own darling —
  but still it's pleasant by the riverside.

My friend is going with them,
and wanted me to go with him —
  though it's pleasant here on the riverbank.

'But,' he said, 'unless your mind
is quite at ease, best stay behind.'
  So it's pleasant watching from the bank.

JOHAN ZORRO

'Let's dance here now, for God agrees . . .'

Let's dance here now, for God agrees,
under these flowering hazel trees,
and if, like us, you're pretty
    and long for a friend to please,
       you'll take a chance,
and underneath the flowering hazel trees
       you'll come and dance.

In God's name now let every young maid
come and dance in the hazel shade,
so when the men applaud we'll know
    we've earned the praise we're paid,
      who, taking our chance,
come to the famous flowering hazel shade
       to dance.

Johan Servando

'To San Servando's hermitage . . .'

To San Servando's hermitage
many today make pilgrimage,
and with such women I too would go,
but all my mother says is: 'No!'
      And why?
            Because my lover will be there.

Oh, I would travel joyfully
in such fine female company,
but my mother does not agree
that such companions are good for me.
      And why?
            Because they'd help me see my friend.

With those women who assemble there
no others on this earth compare,
but I shall not be going with them today,
for nothing on earth will make my mother give way.
      And why?
            Because my lover will be there.

Martín Codax

'In a church in Vigo once . . .'

In a church in Vigo once
I watched a lovely creature dance;
    and fell in love.

In Vigo, and on sacred ground,
the slender figure danced around;
    so I'm in love.

That slender dancer never yet
with a loving friend has met.

That lovely body's never had
a lover either good or bad;
    though I'm in love.

Dancing in Vigo church alone,
never a lover has it known.

In a church in Vigo once
I watched a lovely creature dance;
    and I'm in love.

Dom Johan d'Avoyn

'*My friend, since now you leave me . . .*'

My friend, since now you leave me
and go to live elsewhere,
I pray to God if you return
seeking my time to share
      you never more may get
      one word with me, my pet.

And as you chafe so to be gone,
paying my words no heed,
I pray to God if you return,
lonely and in need,
      you find no way to get
      one word with me, my pet.

Since you won't take into account
the kindnesses we've shared,
I pray to God if you come back
with a speech all prepared
      you find no way to get
      a word with me, my pet.

Since you leave against my pleasure,
and will not heed my word,
why go! But if you come back poor
I call upon the Lord
      to make sure you never get
      another word with me, my pet.

Fernand'Esquyo

'Come, sister, now, let's take our leisure . . .'

Come, sister, now, let's take our leisure
on the shores of the lake where I saw my lover
    go hunting the birds of the air.

Let's go now, sister, and wait together
on the shores of the lake, where I saw my lover
    stalking the birds of the air.

On the shores of the lake, where I saw my lover
walking just now with his bow and quiver,
    seeking the birds of the air.

On the shores of the lake, where I saw my friend
walking just now with his bow in his hand,
    after the birds of the air.

His bow in his hand, he wounds their wings,
but he never hurts the one who sings,
    my lover who hunts the birds of the air.

His bow in his hand, he'll be shooting still,
but the one who sings he may not kill —
    my lover who hunts the birds.

KING DENIS OF PORTUGAL (1261-1325)

'Tell me, flowers of the green pine tree . . .'

Tell me, flowers of the green pine tree,
have you news of my friend to give to me?
    (Dear God, you tell me:
    where is he?)

Tell me, flowers of the green pine bough,
have you word of my lover to give me now?

Have you word of my friend to give to me —
for he swore he would keep me company?

Have you news to tell me about my lover —
who swore he'd stay, and turned deceiver?

'Are you asking me now for news of your friend?
Let me tell you at once that he's safe and sound.

If it's news of your lover you'd have me tell,
be assured by me he's alive and well.

Be assured by me he's safe and sound,
you'll have him back before the time is round.

Let me tell you again he's alive and well,
he'll be back as quick as it takes to tell.'
    (Dear God, you tell me:
    where is he?)

Nuno Fernandez Torneol

'Wake up, my dear, don't sleep through these cold mornings . . .'

Wake up, my dear, don't sleep through these cold mornings,
all the birds in the world are talking of love.
        So let's be happy.

Wake up, my dear, don't sleep in the morning cold,
all the birds in the world of love are singing.

All the birds in the world were talking of love,
both mine for you and yours for me they recounted.

All the birds in the world of love were singing,
on mine for you and yours for me they commented.

Both my love and your love they were recounting,
when you cut down the branches where they lived.

Both my love and your love they were describing,
when you cut down the branches where they alighted.

You cut away the branches where they lived,
and you dried up the fountains where they drank.

You cut away the branches where they alighted,
and you dried up the fountains where they played.
        Let me be happy.

Anonymous

Folksongs

There's great rejoicing in hell:
the scribe has gone to his rest.
The quill and the ink-well
are dancing on his desk.

⌒

This bodhrán no matter how often
I beat it, it never will crack:
for it's made of the very best hide
from off of a gombeen-man's back.

⌒

*Ma mither is sae puir
we hae nae breid tae eat:
she staps ma face wi kisses,
and syne she starts tae greet.*

⌒

You forgot me because I'm poor,
and I you because you're rich;
don't come again to my door
trying to scatter my wits.

⌒

If you leave me, lover,
leave me something of your own:
leave me your cut-throat razor,
to cut the cabbage to the bone.

~

Christian doctrine, Father?
I'd get it all wrong;
but ask me for a song —
and then, by Christ, I'll answer.

~

Up there, I don't know where,
sits some saint, I don't know which,
and for praying who knows what prayer
he's paid — who knows how much?

~

When I see you on the bank of the river
my whole body trembles with cold;
when I see you on top of the mountain
that keeps my whole body warm.

~

Once, to see you,
I opened windows and doors;
now, so as not to see you,
I keep them closed.

~

Only four things do the masters
of every servant require:
don't eat too much, don't drink too much,
work hard, keep smiling.

❧

Farruquiño, you must
become a priest:
though no caress
appease our lust,
I may at least
confess.

❧

I belong to Galicia, and yet I don't,
I wander the world, both heaven and hell;
I'm from Galicia, and yet I'm not:
I know where I'll lay my head tonight,
but where I'll be buried — none can tell.

❧

Mother, I gave you nothing,
you gave me everything!
And now when at last I was starting to help you
they drag me away to fight for the King.

❧

Step it out and step it in,
to the service of the King;
the rich can stay at home,
but we, the poor, must go.

Rosalía de Castro (1837-1885)

'Come all ye men and women . . .'

Come all ye men and women,
come all ye lads and lasses,
and look at the lovely dowry
my father-in-law's providing:
one ancient blanket,
with one red patch upon it,
one blind nanny-goat
with one lame kid,
one decrepit kettle,
and a pot without a handle:
there's a magnificent dowry
for us to set up house with!

Rosalía de Castro

'This man goes and that man goes…'

This man goes and that man goes,
they're going every one;
so you, Galicia, have no men left
to see your work is done.
All you have is orphans,
and lonely, empty fields,
and sons who have no fathers,
and mothers who have no sons.
And you have hearts that suffer
absence long and killing,
widows of the dead and widows of the living
whom none can ever console.

Rosalía de Castro

Castilians of Castile

Castilians of Castile,
    you treat Galicians well:
they leave here full of hope,
    and come back souls in hell.

He went away smiling,
    and came back dying,
the little light of my eyes,
    the little love of my breast.

He was whiter than snow,
    he was gentle and sweet,
I lived for him,
    without him I'd just as soon die.

He went to Castile for bread,
    they gave him weeds instead;
they gave him gall to drink,
    and worry to make his bed.

No trees to give him shelter,
    no shade to let him breathe.
Only the wide plain stretching endless,
    only an endless waste.

Such is *your* affliction, Castile,
    such is *your* birthright.
All you can do with *your* sadness
    is boast with all your might.

Castile, there's nothing
    as ugly as you.
To call you Castile is not enough,
    only hell rings true.

Since my loved one died
    there's none to spare me:
all I have, Castile,
    is the bad milk I bear you.

May it please God, Castilians,
    Castilians I loathe and dread,
sooner my people die than ask
    the likes of you for bread.

They go away poor and come back poor,
    they go away healthy and come back ill,
they leave home like roses
    and come back black as pitch.

Your soul is hard as hell,
    Castilians of Castile,
you've nothing in your breast,
    your heart is made of steel!

Perched on a wisp of straw,
    proud of nothing true,
you think our little sons
    were born to serve you.

Never so crude an idea,
    never so criminal a thought,
by such fatuous teachers
    to such willing learners taught!

Dry sons of the desert,
    what bread you give you poison first;
and a few puddles in the burning ground
    is all you have to cool your thirst.

Why did you go, my own dear love,
    what could you ever hope to gain?
To leave these flowering fields
    for the sad fields bereft of rain!

To leave the clear fountains,
    the murmuring streams,
for dry dust never wet
    by heaven's tears!

My loved one, since you died
    there's nobody can save me;
where once I looked at you,
    all I can see is a grave.

Sad as night itself,
    sick of pain and grief,
I beg God to kill me,
    I've no wish now to live.

But while He's taking His time to kill me,
    Castilians I hate,
I must, for all my weeping,
    sing your shame:

Castilians of Castile,
    you treat Galicians well:
they leave here full of hope
    and come back souls in hell.

Manuel Curros Enríquez (1851-1908)

In Front of an Image of Ignatius Loyola

Putting on a look of mystical delight,
but with anger in your breast and sleep in your eyes,
I've got your measure, you whitewashed Fury,
you brazen Catholic, hirpling virtue.

Turning her back on the Gospel's loving law,
the Bride of the Song of Songs, debasing herself,
consorted with the Devil and from such congress
you, you gloating parasite, got born.

What are you doing on that altar, plundering honours,
you the begetter of all intolerance,
you that have earned only curses?

You that made a tyrant of Christ,
magistrates of assassins and bully-boys,
and of God himself a strangler of human thought?

Celso Emilio Ferreiro (1914-1979)

Once

There once was a man
who never said mine.
He knocked on the doors of the world,
he called on my heart.
The words he spoke
were like doves.
Things when he drew near them
grew white.
His eyes gave birth to a dawn
like a river of light
or a distant ocean of seagulls.
That man
had a balm of love
for this my nameless
grief.

Celso Emilio Ferreiro

Letter to My Wife

My dear, you must not forget there are words
it's a sin to say these days.
Words you must not pronounce,
nor even think, let alone
touch, praise, or write . . .
much less shout.
Wife, take note and never forget:
you must not say freedom, that sad word;
it carries the death-penalty, the skull.
If you really love me never say
that stupid word,
it has teeth, and bites like a wolf.
Don't even say
any of its derivatives,
however distant and vague
their etymological connection may be,
as, for example, free love,
freebooter, free-wheeling, free trade.

Instead say chains, long live,
yes sir, thanks very much, God reward you.

Then you'll see how happy we'll be!

Celso Emilio Ferreiro

Freely

We wanted freely
to eat our daily bread. Freely
to bite into it, chew it, digest it fearlessly,
freely talking, singing on the banks
of rivers on their way to the free sea.
Freely, freely
we wanted only
to be freely men, to be stars,
to be sparks in the great fire of the world,
to be ants, birds, kittens,
in this Noah's ark we travel in.
We wanted to smile freely,
to speak to God in the passing wind —
the long wind of plains and woods —
fearless, darkless, chainless,
sinless, freely, freely,
like daybreak and foam.
Like the wind.
But our difficult love broke —
frail dream glass —
on a rock of cries
and now we are no more than shadows.

Celso Emilio Ferreiro

Orphan Child against a Background of Horses

The horses of the night went by
and the dawn came.
Mother,
this is the land of tears.
The horses of the night
went by at a gallop.
Mother,
this is the land of lament.
Like a solitary firefly
I would like to be
blind with light on the roads.
The horses of the night went by
like a black wind.
Mother,
the horses left me an orphan.

Celso Emilio Ferreiro

The Mad Dog

Like a mad dog on the roads
terror walks loose through the world.
As if a black wind placed
its crow wings over
the brows of frightened men.
An ice of winter in the open
paralyzes clocks, pierces throats
and covers words in veils of anguish.
A great telescope keeps watch on us
like a Cyclops' eye
following our steps,
in ambush for us wherever we go,
waiting and watching from all the windows,
from all the towers,
from all the voices that speak to us.
The night's an impassive microphone
absorbing the beating of our breasts
like a dark spy attentive
to our most secret thoughts.
All things become unconfessable;
behind every corner a suspicion,
a doubt behind every shadow,
and fear, fear, fear,
a deep well of fear,
a mirror of cold water
where terror eternally looks at itself.

Celso Emilio Ferreiro

Stretched out beside the Sea

I speak the proletarian language of my people
because I want to, because I enjoy speaking it,
because it comes from inside me, from the deep
corrosive sadness I feel when I see so many
cretinous uprooted little time-servers
who the minute they put a collar-and-tie round their necks
cannot any longer share in their forebears' love,
or speak the mother tongue,
the tongue of their own dear dead ones,
and be, with head high,
mariners and farmers of the language,
oar and plough, harrow and prow.

I speak it because I enjoy it, because I want
to be with my own people,
beside good men who have suffered too long
a history chanted in a tongue not their own.

I'm not speaking for the proud,
I'm not speaking for the powerful,
the snobbish, the empty, the stupid:
I speak for those who grimly put up with
constant lies and injustice;
for people who sweat and weep
a daily lament of butterflies,
of wind and fire on their naked eyes.
How could I keep my words apart
from the suffering people of this world?
And it's in this world you're living,
my country, my cradle, Galicia,
gentle agony of Spain,
stretched out beside the sea, that journey.

Celso Emilio Ferreiro

The Kingdom

In those days
when the animals could speak,
to say freedom wasn't sad,
to say truth was like a river,
to say love,
to say friend,
was like naming the springtime.
Outrage was something no one knew about.
When the animals talked
men sang at evening,
doves of light, finches of dreaming.
To say yours or mine was pointless,
to say sword was forbidden,
to say prison was only a word
devoid of meaning, an air that hurt
people's hearts.

When,
when did we lose
that great Kingdom?

Celso Emilio Ferreiro

City Cemetery

The pride of the powerful reaches the graveyards,
it turns into Corinthian marbles
and proprietary bronzes.
    We must plant this placard in the world:
    There are first-class dead and second-class dead
    and dead with nowhere to fall down dead.
A rich man's skeleton
is worth three skeletons
of simple men who get paid on Saturdays
for sweating out their dreams and hopes.
The powerful dead
arrive at the graveyard with dress-circle tickets
and are ushered to an urn of segregated marble,
imagining the trumpets of the last judgement
will blow exclusively for them
a beautifully florid fanfare.
    One day we'll dispossess them of this offensive earth
    and make one single egalitarian tomb.
We'll throw the noxious marbles into the sea
and melt down the proud bronzes in the fire.
We'll send the heirs of the proud the bones of their forebears
—
they can quote them on the Stock Exchange
along with nitrate, steel, coal and copper,
and so they can go on living, as always, on their rents.

Celso Emilio Ferreiro

Old Workman Speaking

Now I'm taking the sun. But up to now
I worked for fifty years without a break.
I ate my bread sweating day after day
in ceaseless labour.
I spent time like my Saturday wages;
Spring went by, Winter came.
I gave the boss the flower of my strength
and my youth. I have nothing.
The boss is rich at my expense,
I, at his, am old.
Come to think of it, the boss owes me everything.
I don't owe him
even the sun I'm taking now.

While I take it, I'm waiting.

CELSO EMILIO FERREIRO

'Death is like a tree...'

Death is like a tree
planted with us, born to us
when we are born, with the first
tear in our eyes.
A tree born to us on the left
of a long road through the night.
I'm sure I'll see it when I die:
a lone tree — with no leaves —
rising in front of me towards the sky
like hands joined in prayer
in the far depths of a plain.
A tree alone,
naked against the night,
growing, it'll keep on growing
till it fills my eyes with ants.

Celso Emilio Ferreiro

Long Night of Stone

No meio do caminho tinha uma pedra
tinha uma pedra no meio do caminho
tinha uma pedra
no meio do caminho tinha uma pedra
— Carlos Drummond de Andrade

The roof is made of stone.
The shadows, the walls,
are of stone.
A stone floor, stone bars.
The doors,
chains,
air,
windows,
glances
are stone.
The hearts of men
waiting far away
are also
made
of stone.
And I, dying
in this long night
of stone.

In the middle of the road I had a stone
I had a stone in the middle of the road
I had a stone
in the middle of the road I had a stone

Uxío Novoneyra (1930-1999)

The Owl

Owl singing in the quiet night
in the shadow of mingled boughs,
you turn these city trees
into an old wood where I always was.
Your song knows nothing of the houses
heaped up all around us,
so I can forget they were built.

You and I weren't made
to live here.
We're both from a long way off
and someday we'll go back there,
where our mystery may be adjusted.

You'll go after I do,
some night when nobody is watching,
in this city of clouds and slow bells.

Uxío Novoneyra

'To hear the cows grazing in the evening . . .'

To hear the cows grazing in the evening
in the mountain silence
is almost like watching, in the valley,
the water flowing over the weir.

Xosé Luis Méndez Ferrín (1938-)

Tale

Galicia was a pure valley or hollow
of dense green, moist smoke.
Galicia was the most naked plain,
inert mist over a pool of mud.

Galicia was a kindly wind but keen,
that sheltered everything within it.
Galicia was a tree with leaves
each hour a little more ingrown.

Galicia was a hundred forebears' clay
still unavenged, dumb echoes moving us.
Galicia was a sea so perfectly dense
it had no light, no flavour of men.

Galicia was a homeland of work
never finished because of the ships.
Galicia was a man without a head.
Once it was Galicia, a narrow hope.

Arcadio López-Casanova (1942-)

'They were all called up . . .'

They were all called up.
They were told: 'Spain needs soldiers.'
And they answered the call.
I write down their names. In memoriam.
Cándido López, Miguel Díaz,
Antón Parapar, Xesús Castro,
Manuel Rodríguez, they were men
from the Páramo — the waste land.
They knew nothing. Each one accepted
his rifle, his helmet,
and, in single file, off they went.
I repeat: they knew nothing.
They went quietly.
As one man they left their lands,
their fields,
for other lands and other
machine-gunned deserts.
That's war.
This time it lasted three years.
Not one came back. They all
died far away from Galicia.
They're unknown heroes.
They died
not knowing why they fought.
Their country was the earth
furrowed by the plough.
They knew no Spains
instilled at gunpoint.
That's all.
I bear witness, add nothing.
In memoriam. Here
I set down their names.

Emilio Araúxo (1946-)

Name

They ask him where he's from.
He names a village.
In Ourense.
A winter evening.
A village name
resounding a little
in a hospital ward.
A long name,
full of names,
full of music
and sunlit pain.
The sun in smithereens
like a piece of bread
on the river of forgetting.

Emilio Araúxo

'a stone scored by a tile . . .'

a stone scored by a tile
by a tile that fell from a roof

as if it had shit
a stone growing

a stone growing
like milk on the fire
a stone going mad to grow

Emilio Araúxo

October

Chestnuts that fall
from the eyes of the dead
and romp their way into the fire
where they start to grow again
for you to eat.

CHUS PATO (1955-)

from *Heloisa*

How Oedipus came to be king of the seas and Antigone
learnt
the language of birds.

Black is the splendour of the stars
black the five-petal rose you lavish upon me.

Beggars drown in your eyes
crows' wings unfold from a woman's shoulders.

The name you engraved on my skin
even today still sparkles
scorches
burns.

Lupe Gómez (1972-)

'I speak and write . . .'

I speak and write
Galician,
like a child
in a small village
where the world stops
and the women
walk naked,
with flowing locks
and bodies free as air.

ANONYMOUS (14TH/15TH CENTURY)

Folksong

St John's Day in the morning,
                just as the day was dawning,
Jesus Christ went walking
                beside the fountain clear;
with his voice he said then,
                from his mouth was heard then:
'This water here is blessèd
                and blest the fountain here.'
That made the king's daughter,
                from her high tower listening,
pull on her silken stockings,
                put on her shoes of silver,
pick up her golden pitcher,
                and go to the spring for water.
When she'd gone only half way
                she met the Virgin Mary,
and asked her, greatly daring:
                'Must I soon be wed?'
'Soon you shall be married,
                my lovely lucky young lady,
three noble sons will grace you,'
                the Virgin Mary said:
'One'll be Cardinal in Braga,
                another a Bishop in Rome,
but the youngest and the last one
                shall serve me here at home.'
Happy was that king's daughter
                when she went to the spring
                for water!

CARLOS DRUMMOND DE ANDRADE (1902-1987)

An Ox Looks at Human Beings

So delicate they are (a shrub is more robust)
and they keep on running from side to side
and they're always forgetting something. They lack
some essential attribute, that's certain, though at times
they do appear noble and grave. Astonishingly grave,
even sinister. Poor things, you'd think they never hear
either the song of the air or the secrets of hay,
nor do they seem to perceive what is visible
and common to all of us, in space. And they look sad
and in the trail of sadness arrive at cruelty.
All their expression is in their gaze — and it vanishes
at the drop of an eyelid, or a shadow.
Nothing in their hair, in their extremities of such
    inconceivable fragility,
and they're so unmountainous,
and all that dryness and all those re-entrances and how
incapable of organizing themselves into calm shapes,
permanent and necessary. They have, perhaps,
a certain melancholy grace (for a minute) and so may win
    forgiveness
for the troublesome bustle, the translucent
inner emptiness that makes them so poor, so needy,
emitting absurd sounds of anguish: desire, love, jealousy,
sounds that smash to pieces and fall in the fields
like afflicted stones and burn the grass and water,
and after that it's difficult for us
to ruminate our truth.

MÁRIO ANTÓNIO (FERNANDES DE OLIVEIRA) (1934-1989)

'Moonlight on the jetty at Maianga . . .'

Moonlight on the jetty at Maianga
A song walks on the air:
'Rotting bananas bring nobody luck . . .'
Girls falling in love in the timber-yards
Old women sitting on mats telling old stories
Men getting drunk in pubs
And the immigrants from the islands . . .
The immigrants from the islands
With brine in their hair
The immigrants from the islands
Talking of sorcerers and calm seas
And playing violins
And wearing, each one, a knife in his belt . . .
Children singing
Girls falling in love
Old wives' tales
The mysteries of men

Workingmen forgetting in pubs
Immigrants with knives in their belts
And the sound a fiddle makes
And the hymns of the missionaries

    men
    men
    the tragedies of men

Anonymous (15th century)

'Climbing into my lover's bed . . .'

Climbing into my lover's bed
I put out my hand and touched her side.
That woke her up so she cried out:
'How did *you* get in, you backsliding cur?'

'Through the door,' said I,
'you are my life, my love, be kind to me.'
'Oh well, now that you're here,' said she,
'strip off, lie down, come close.'

After our sport was done
I wanted to get up and dress:
but she said, 'Stay a bit longer,
there's no knowing when you'll come back.'

Torquato Tasso (1544-1595)

'The streams and woods fall silent . . .'

The streams and woods fall silent,
no wave disturbs the sea.
In caves the wind has called a truce,
and the white moon brings a deep silence
into the dark night,
where we in secret share
the sweet delights of love.
Don't speak, or breathe, my dear,
our kisses, like my sighs, must make no sound.

Umberto Saba (1883-1957)

The Goat

I spoke to a goat.
She was tied up alone in a field.
Fed up with grass,
rain-soaked, bleating.
That plaint was a brother
of my own suffering, so I
replied, at first for fun
and then because suffering's eternal,
it has one voice, and never alters.
That voice I heard
sobbing in a lonely goat.
In a goat with a Jewish face
I heard all hurt complain,
all other life.

SANDRO PENNA (1906-1977)

'To *a latrine cool in the railway station* . . .'

To a latrine cool in the railway station
I come down from the scorching hill.
My skin is drunk with dust and sweat.
The sun is still singing in my eyes.
To the shining white porcelain
I abandon body and soul.

Elio Vittorini (1908-1966)

from *Conversation in Sicily*

1

A small old man with a tall
wooden stick full of knots,
a snake's head the knob of it —
when suddenly I noticed
green in the serpent's mouth,
three little leaves of an orange-twig,
and the old man noticed me noticing,
and laughed and took the orange-twig
and put it in his own mouth,
his mouth like the slit in a money-box —
his own head a snake's head.

2

A terrible summer, my mother said.
Not a shadow for miles.
The cicadas bursting in the sun,
every thing turned into sun.
A terrible summer, she said.
The snails cracked open by the sun.

Then I asked her
was it morning or evening
the stranger came?
I think it was evening, she said.
There were no wasps,
there were no flies,
there was nothing.
It must have been evening.

I'd been baking, she said.
So that was it —
for miles and miles the smell of dead snakes in the sun,
and then, all of a sudden, all round a house,
a smell of bread just-baked!
I'd been baking bread, she said.
Then I was washing, beside the well.
I always washed in the evening.

The wanderer, just back from a war,
had walked for miles and miles
through a land with no water,
no villages;
the only dwelling he passed
a large farmstead
the dogs allowed no wanderer near.

He was still wearing his old uniform,
but stript of stars.
He walked in his bare feet,
boots dangling down his back,
laced around his neck.

By that day
he'd walked for forty-eight hours,
not drinking, not eating.
As he was telling her his story
he was drinking a pail of water she had given him.
Then she brought him bread:
breathing in that new air,
smelling that still fresh bread,
God be praised! he said.

He came back often,
always when her own man was away at work
    on the railway.
He was hungry and thirsty
for more than bread.
My mother gave him what he needed.

He brought me little presents, she said.
Once,
he brought a honeycomb:
its perfume filled the whole house
with the smell of honey.

Then he stopped coming.
I asked why.
Once the sulphur-miners went on strike
and even the country folk rebelled as well.
The railwaymen didn't come out.
The state forces killed more than a hundred.

You think, I said, your wanderer
was one of those?
I do, she said,
for why else
would he give up coming to me?

She'd nothing more to do in the kitchen.
She sat quiet,
                    tranquil,
smoothing her dress.

NELO RISI (1920-)

'The maxim that torture degrades . . .'

The maxim that torture degrades
the torturer has now had its day —
torture degrades the innocent victim.

Torturers will never be punished enough;
we can only hope the torturer's son
may be innocent enough to deserve torture.

Franco Loi (1930-)

'Through tired air we go, filled up with nothing . . .'

Through tired air we go, filled up with nothing,
tho' unbeknownst to ourselves we're full of words,
we go as if searching for our own shadow,
then we get lost, but one of these days we'll find
our shadow there before us, entirely empty —
air in the soul, and no more searching.

FRANCO LOI

'*I want to say a prayer to you, God . . .*'

I want to say a prayer to you, God,
a short one, as best I can —
but you must listen quietly. . .
Let death, for us, be like life
when it trembles in our hands at dawn,
or like when evening comes into the heart
and we tremble to it like branches.

FRANCO LOI

'*Was it here, in Milan — I can't remember . . .*'

Was it here, in Milan — I can't remember —
the timeless air
of that piazza?
I tried to round a corner and in the rain
people passed by like the wind.
Around that corner a white shirt
seemed to be waiting for me —
but no, there was nothing.
The timeless piazza, an exhausted woman,
and men going by, locked into their feelings.
I don't know where I was. I remember a bench,
and I was walking among the people,
and the corner I never rounded
was life heard from afar.

AMEDEO GIACOMINI (1940-)

Mad Toni

Eight litres of wine a day,
too much even for a saint,
or one who wanted to invent a way of dying . . .
There you sat with your wine,
all on your own, with your silence . . .
(Every now and then you wept,
watching your paunch grow.)
I don't know why you did it,
you drove yourself mad for nothing,
you my bowels, father,
Mad Toni, always drunk
and always in despair.

Giacomo Noventa (1898-1960)

'What's beyond . . .'

What's beyond
the sky, father?
Sky, my son.
And beyond that?
More sky.
And beyond that?
Worse luck,
God.

Virgilio Giotti (1885-1957)

The Street

I look at a street in my city,
a street I must have passed a thousand times,
and it's as if I've never seen it before.
The pale yellow facades, the shops,
a bar, a few cars, the odd passerby.
Yes, it's just like our life: lived,
soon over, and never really known.

Donnchadh Mór Ó Dálaigh (*died* 1244)

O, One Son of God

O, One Son of God who died on the top of the Tree,
the heart in your side torn by the hand of the Blind,
the blood of your wound coming down to the ground
    in a pool,
in the shade of your gaze take us yourself to Paradise.

Jesus, bright King, our Father and our Lamb,
who gave the true blood of your dear heart to buy us hard,
be my shelter, be my company, be near me every hour,
when I'm lying down or getting up, when I'm standing
    or sleeping.

Put down my vengeance, my anger, and my hatred,
and drive away from me accursèd thoughts.
Let a small drop of your blest Holy Ghost come down
to release my heart that's as hard as a rock.

PÁDRAIGÍN HAICÉAD (1600-1654)

After Breaking My Own Foot in France

My little wandering limb the splint must thole:
it brings me nearer my dear one to console.
How poor a friend I'd be, examined home,
if, his bone broken, I broke not my own.

Haicéad wrote this poem soon after hearing that a friend in Ireland
had broken his.

Caitlín Maude (1941-1982)

'I long for a rhyme of health . . .'

I long for a rhyme of health
a small fresh syllable
a poultice of words
to put the soul right
and make the body strong.

I long for a rhyme
to put the soul right.

PAUL VAN OSTAIJEN (1896-1928)

from *Asta*

Asta Nielsen
Asta
astra
star
queen Our dear Lady
Our Lady of Denmark
we bear you under baldaquins
broad Host.
        You
The greatest comfort of tired men
'according to well-informed sources in Paris London Berlin
Petrograd Rome'
day in day out
paternoster of news
litany of starving cigarettes
as out of the light came darkness
and out of the darkness light

Lightning
Starring Asta Nielsen
Queen of the Stock Exchange
Eskimonogirl Carmen First-Class, Death Comes to Seville
I can still see your hips moving
and your lips biting the soft flower
full is the fall
            of your hands
                  and how you come!
vous Voilà!
Asta
astra
happy humanity
ma bien-aimée

You know how to make an entrance
and all of a sudden the operator's throbbing
the screen's in perpetual equilibrium
because of *You*
Immanence
Cinemabalance
You
Asta
Our prayer

O sacred film-star-balance
        pray for us
poor cinemaseekers
soft hands' clean fall
        pray for us (tired men)
good whore's laughter
        pray for us (tired loins)
laughter pray for us
        the unrefreshed

Asta
greater than all the stars together
pray for us
who can even do it without stars
Asta
greater than the Sun
since the invention of electricity
Asta
greater than the Moon
pray for us
who lack the Sun, the Moon, the Stars
but never lack the cinema
soft hands, aperitifs

Asta
deliver us not into sentimentality
but give us this day the objectivity
of your delicate feet
Asta
deliver us from gaslight
in this electric era

Asta
do us a good turn
and go on starring in films
go on playing with your feet
but not with ours

De Profundis Cla-ma-vi
I'm not fooling:
You *are* our daily bread
more than Schopenhauer Bergson or the Past Pupils' Union

Big passive Asta
your broad face
broad mouth
spacious cherry
objective lust

Asta
2 boxers batter each other in each man of us
and each one always knocks the other out
Asta
We're boxing for *you*
the blood is dripping down our faces
but the sacrifice is never great enough

               drink
                       our
                               blood
                                        aperitif
You're a good woman
Your hips are only divine
Liszt
Asta

Hendrik Marsman (1899-1940)

Farewell

Sleep with darkness, woman
sleep with the night

our deepest embraces
have killed the dream

dark and pitiless
are blood and sex

sleep with darkness, woman
sleep with the night.

Judith Herzberg (1934-)

Living Life to the Full

Shall we
said she
lie down together
in a big bed
in a hotel-
room
wearing pyjamas
and let
the page-boy
bring us
a cake?

Judith Herzberg

Old Woman

The fantasies I had before I was sick!
Philosophy, polyandry, Andalusia,
and what not, but now? I'd like to hang
the leaves back again on the branches.
Twice a day I waver down the hall.

Joris Iven (1942-)

The House on the Lake

Of the many houses I live in
Not one is mine.
My house is the house on the lake.
Next to my house a lake,
Next to my lake another lake.
My house stands in a wood.
Next to my house no other house.
My house stands in the wood alone.
And of the many women I possess
Not one is mine.
My woman lives in the house
On the lake.
My woman lives in the house
In the wood.
In my house in the wood
On the lake
I live alone.
Of all the houses I live in
Not one is mine
And of all the lakes near my house
Not one is mine.
In the whole wood
Not one tree is mine.
And of all the women not one is mine.
I own nothing
And my woman,
My woman sleeps her sleep
In the house I live in.

(Luc de Clapiers, Marquis de) Vauvenargues
   (1715-1747)

'The contemplator, softly couched . . .'

The contemplator, softly couched
in a well-carpeted room,
inveighs against the soldier,
who spends the winter nights beside a river,
and stays awake, in silence,
to keep their country safe.

Jean-Joseph Rabéarivelo (1901-1937)

from *Old Songs from Imerina*

24

Those waters north of my grandfather's house: they never foam
before they overflow; and ebbing still conceal their sandy bed.
    Family discussions are over: now the lovers can talk.

29

— Kestrel's egg in the very heart of the ravine, you know I've
asked you to come back; and so has The-man-who-knows-
how-to-console-himself.
— Let them all learn how to console themselves, the libertines,
my heart of compassion is gone!
— There are twelve hills: go and play the flute among them,
play the fiddle there! But you, my spirit, force me to come back
for fear I'm driven mad by a woman who doesn't miss me!

32

— Who's that north of the fire?
— It's me, The-woman-with-a-silver-face-and-a-noble-way-
of-walking.
— Who's that west of the fire?
— It's me, The-woman-in-blue-and-black-whom-a-thousand-
men-can't-have.
— I trust that nothing I do will seem offensive to your ways,
my Lady, so you won't feel like cursing me. But I'm going to
put the one in the house out and bring in the one who's in the
courtyard.
— In that case, my Lord, do tell her to come in quietly; for my

part, I shall invite The-man-who-is-hard-to-give-up!

33

— Who's that north of the fire?
— It's me, The-girl-with-a-golden-face.
— Who's that west of the fire?
— It's me, The-elegant-woman-with-crisp-hair-who-chases-compunction-away.
— Her two hands are full of oranges; I'd ask her for some, but I'm shy of her. All the same, if I listened too much to my shame, the water would reach my mouth.
— Whoever listens too much to his shame will have nothing; whoever fears his responsibilities will never have his desire!

44

A single shot rings out in the Village of the Gods. The Giant's Village isn't far away, but nobody hears it there. Where-the-riverbanks-are-long, armfuls of space unfurl: my father and mother always have some money, and when my lover and I are sleeping together, nobody ever disturbs us.

Anonymous

Folksongs

I watched her long journey,
she rode in the hearse,
the single hand that dangled out
I knew at once for hers.

❧

I'd like to be the ground where
they put you down for good;
I'd hold you in my arms till
wine turned wood.

❧

I gave a grave a kiss;
the stone broke in two:
that's where they'd buried
the one that bore you.

I gave a grave a kiss;
the stone broke in three:
that's where they'd buried
the one that bore me.

Transcribed in 1899 by Darío Regoyos (1857-1913)
and Emile Verhaeren (1855-1916)

Antonio Machado (1875-1939)

'A sailor made a garden on the shore . . .'

A sailor made a garden on the shore,
setting himself to every garden chore.
And when the whole garden was in full flower,
the gardener went off to sea once more.

León Felipe (1884-1968)

Communion

Somewhere it is said that God eats men
and men one day shall eat God.

And it is also written
that man is no more than a fish
in a sea of ignorance and weeping.

And somewhere else again the question is asked:
Why is He sitting up there
on a high precipice of frozen cloud,
that Great Fisherman?
What's He at there
with His bait,
His hook
and His long fishing-rod —
that Great Fisherman?

Is man no more than a fish,
a fish for the flames of hell
though later, 'pure and golden',
he'll be eaten, up there,
by that Great Fisherman?

So here and now the fish — the man —
stands up for himself and says:
Some day I'll swallow the sea . . .
all the water in the sea . . .
all the dark in the sea like a black pearl . . .
some day I'll swallow the sea . . .
all the water in the sea . . .
all the bitterness in the sea like a single tear . . .
leaving exposed

the bait,
the hook
and the long fishing-rod
of that Great Fisherman —
all His lies and His truth!
Then I'll sit down to weep on the last dry rock in the world,
to weep, and go on weeping,
until I've once more filled the earth
with another vast sea,
much blacker and much bitterer than our sea now . . .
another sea that reaches to the skies,
inundates the stars
and drowns that Great Fisherman
with His bait,
His hook
and His long fishing-rod.
Then
I shall be the fisherman
and God, the Great Fish, surprised and caught.
On that day Man — all humanity — will eat God.
That'll be the day, the Great Day of the true,
the glorious
holy communion.

José Moreno Villa (1887-1955)

Ripe Voice

Lend me your green cane.
Take my pomegranate stick.

Can't you see the sky is red,
the fields yellow?

That oranges taste of roses,
and roses of the human body?

Lend me your green cane,
take my pomegranate stick.

José Bergamín (1895-1983)

Rhymes

Your voice makes the silence more silent,
your gaze darkens the dark.
And all that you touch with your hands
turns into shadow and smoke.

In your naked body the bright
flame of your blood makes sleep
more sleep, and the world's
fabled awakening more dreamt of.

I dreamt I was weeping,
then knew on awaking
I can no longer weep
except when I'm dreaming.

I saw a shadow on the wall
and another shadow at the window.
I knew that at the door
yet another shadow was waiting.

My words are made of air.
Perhaps that's why
they reach no ear.

How often my hands
touched the heavens,
while feeling my heart
burn in the flames of hell.

The bullfighter dying of fear
is the one who bullfights best:
because he has killed his shadow
and only his light is left.

Emilio Prados (1899-1962)

Sleeping on the Grass

Everyone comes to give me advice.
I'm sleeping beside a well.

They all come and tell me:
Life is passing you by,
and you're stretched out on the grass
in the dwindling light of dusk,
concerned only to watch
the evening star in its trembling birth
or listen to the small sound
of water between the trees.

And you're stretched out on the grass:
when already your hair
begins to feel
closer and colder than ever
the caress and kiss
of the moon's faithful
dreaming hand.

But you stretch out on the grass:
though you can scarcely
feel in your side
the moist heat
of gathering seed
or the bitter rustling
of a dying rose.

And you lie there on the grass:
though the wind can scarce
contain its vehemence

when it sees in ruins
the walls of your back,
and even the sun can't be bothered
to raise your blood from silence.

Everyone comes and tells me:
Life is passing you by.
You come from a shore
where rosemary grows with lavender
between the jasmine and the snow, undying,
and the sea was all foam
that brought you here
to speak to us.
But you go to sleep on the grass.

They all keep telling me:
You sleep on the ground
and your heart is bleeding,
drop by drop,
quite painless now, above your sleep,
as in the most secret
part of the garden, at night,
a violet dies, bereft of scent.
Everyone comes to give me advice.
I'm sleeping beside a well.

But when a friend
comes to join me and, without a word,
gives me a hug in the shadows,
I bring him with me to the edge
where we can watch together as they weep,
in those deep waters,
the moon and its reflexion

which later drown
like a golden stone
in the cold autumn of death.

Luis Cernuda (1902-1963)

An Idle Man

With men like you commerce would be
a light thing and so pure that, without sweat,
buying nobody's blood, it would leave the earth
her poisons intact. But for your poverty
commerce could smooth out a way.

In southern summer evenings, through
a clear city, the streets alone,
you'd carry in a basket garlands of jasmine
and magnolias, hiding in a fragrant nest of green leaves
their whiteness, like doves' wings.

If a woman behind the bars of her window
at street-level wanted a flower's fresh gala
for her dark grace, to wear in her hair, on her breast,
where it must look like snow on the earth,
she'd leave, in exchange, a coin in your hand.

So, when evening set, you'd be able
to drink the blond warmth of a transparent wine,
biting the delight of bread or fruit,
and then, silent, stretched out beside the river,
watch, in the deep night, the stars breathing.

MANUEL ALTOLAGUIRRE (1905-1959)

Trine

I want to live for ever
in a tower with three windows,
where three different lights
give one light to my soul.

Three people and one light
in that high tower.

Down here, among men,
where good and evil contend,
two means discord,
two stands for menace.

I want to live for ever
in a tower with three windows.

OCTAVIO PAZ (1914-1998)

Body at Hand

And the shadows opened again, and showed a body:
your hair, dense autumn, sun-water
falling; your mouth and the white discipline of its cannibal
    teeth, imprisoned in flames;
your skin like bread scarcely golden yet, your eyes of burnt
    sugar,
places where no time passes,
glens known only to my lips,
mountain-pass of the moon rising to your throat between
    your breasts,
your neck: that frozen waterfall and the high plateau of your
    belly,
the endless beach of your side.

Your eyes are the fixed gaze of the tiger,
and then, a minute later, the moist eyes of a dog.

There are always bees in your hair.

Your back flows tranquil under my eyes,
like the back of a river in firelight.

Sleeping waters, day and night, lap your clay waist
and, on your shores, limitless like the sands of the moon,
the wind blows through my mouth and that long plaint covers
    with its two grey wings
the night of the bodies,
as eagle-shadow covers the lonely desert.

Your toenails are made of summer crystal.

Between your legs there's a well of sleeping water,
bay where the sea falls quiet at night, black horse of foam,
cave in the foothills hiding a treasure,
mouth of the oven where the Host is baked,
smiling lips half-open, fearful,
nuptials of light and shade, of the seen and the unseen
(where the flesh awaits its resurrection and the day of
    everlasting life).

Homeland of the blood,
the only country I know and that knows me,
the only fatherland I believe in,
the only door to infinity.

Anonymous (First half of the 14th Century)

'I'd a right to be won . . .'

I'd a right to be won
for a wife, or have fun
with a kind lover-man;
but I'm all undone
since they made me a nun.

They sinned a great sin
when they put me in
and held me down
to be a nun.
May God disdain
their pleas and chain
them deep in pain.
I was the right eejit —
for if I'd known
what it's like to be a nun,
I'd never have gone in —
no, not even
for all the gold in Heaven.

Roiç de Corella (*c.*1438-1497)

'*The fierce north wind will rise and rage . . .*'

The fierce north wind will rise and rage
and all at once the heavens fall to bits,
the fire in the sky freeze,
the centre of the earth climb into sight,
the moon turn a smudge of blood,
and the sun, quenched, lose all its shape,
before I ever serve you again. I pray
my body, from the slenderest hair down to the nails,
may shatter into pieces before your eyes
and, turned to dust, find no burial place,
nor the world receive my scurrying ashes;
nor anybody busy his tongue to tell
my cursèd soul to 'rest in peace' —
if God permits your eyes to see my eyes again.
But if in fact I once more call you Lady
let not the day of my birth be found in the year,
let not my name, execrated by all,
find one soul in the world to murmur it,
and so, completely scoured from human thought,
my being, like the wind, be gone.
What I based my life on, let all hold false
and nothing of me remain on earth; but if
by bad luck a scrap of my body survives
may the wild animals eat it.
Let each man take one tiny grain of me
and make a thousand places share my tomb;
and so when the world ends my flesh not be found,
nor I, ever, be made to rise again.

Roiç de Corella

'You'll have upon your tomb, in golden letters . . .'

You'll have upon your tomb, in golden letters,
my death as your most glorious triumph, plain
for all to read how you drove me out of my time,
killing, with your purity, my dead life.
And I, carved in marble at your feet,
kneeling in so simple a way
that all must cry out, with their eyes full of tears:
'A cruel virtue this, that could not yield
to such a humble plea: this man was a phoenix
of true love. No other loved so much.'

While you, full-length in alabaster carved
straight from the life, image of Helen's own self,
must wear an emerald upon your ring-finger,
your other hand clutching a branch of honesty,
on which a turtle-dove shall moan full sore;
and, written on green lilies, these words:
'If anyone claims that virtue must be lost,
for you alone I might have longed to lose it;
but evil may not conceive
hopes of bearing good.'

But since, for fear of sinning against virtue,
I could not give you back your life again,
I won't hide from you how I learned to suffer,
praying God to keep safe from the deep dungeon
your spirit, that was so like mine.
My stone shape will change, even move,
when people read these words upon the tomb:

'Thinking of me, you learned to weep.'
And my sad life won't hurt me any longer,
for I could spend it all and only for you.

Anonymous (18th Century)

The Abduction

At the big tower, at the small tower:
Pepa whom everyone loves;
the rose is lovely, the rose bush lovelier still;
everyone loves her so much, no one'll marry her.
She goes to the river, to wash an apron,
to look pretty on Christmas Day.
While she's washing it, her sweetheart passes:
'What are you doing here, Pepa?'
'I'm washing a skirt, also an apron,
to look pretty on Christmas Day.'
He lifts her up on his horse's back;
the saddle is green, the horse is white.
Along the roads of Lleida, the girl goes sobbing and sighing:
'What are you weeping for, Pepa? What makes you cry so
   much?'
'It's for my parents I'm weeping, for my brothers I weep;
they're decent folk: this will kill them.'
'If they die, then let them die, others can bury them,
the tombs are new, they'll be the first to fill them;
at each corner of each tomb, a wreath may rest,
and friars and priests can pray for them.'

Joan Maragall (1860-1911)

The Boats

One by one, like virgins dancing,
the boats glide into the sea;
the sails open like wings to the sun,
and move seaward on roads
no one else knows.

Blue sky, blue sea; deserted strand
yellow with sun . . . The sea sings into your ear
as you wait the return, in splendour,
at sunset, of the first boat,
emerging aromatic from the sea.

JOSEP CARNER (1884-1970)

Heat

A cluster of fennel
growing by the road,
a vine tired
of summer dust.

A swallow in flight,
a setter sleeping near
a croft rich
in heart's-ease.

And the proud, sensitive
poplar's joy
burning alive
out over the river.

JOSEP CARNER

Fidelity

If a hot sword blinded me
I'd still know every house in my native village:
God's house by the smell of incense,
the miller's by a smell of mint;
and all three bakeries by a smell of bread;
scenting lavender writhing on a fire,
I'd say to myself: 'That must be Paul's place,
he's been laid up now for twenty years';
a smell of singeing would betray
the vet's house.

If, losing memory, I lost my way,
only to end up here, some night,
all the streets would cry to me:
'Here is the ancient square the people dance in,
here the bowling lane, so full of noise,
and here the corner where
your sweetheart, sunset-blushing, came to meet you.
Here's the marketplace, and here the wash house,
and now, the rank, black street of pubs;
and here the teeming high-road, where your father
on feast days, when you were small, sat you up
in a donkey-creel, to take you to the vineyard,
smooth-hearted over tracks of jolting peace.

If misadventure set my wits astray,
in the great, gleaming, treacherous towns,
you'd take my soul in your arms, not scolding, not making
a fuss, and that restraint would bring me back to sense.
I'd hear the girls talking on the bridge,
and near the peace of night a blackbird singing.
A sound of leaves could bring sleep back

to eyes no longer stung by sparks of anguish.
In front of embankments, landmarks, I would feel
my bad memory drop, like a mist, away;
you'd resurrect in me, at every plant,
every pebble in the road, an old instinctive skill.
And near a mountain stream that glides through fern,
catching sight of you decked out in wheat and pasture,
I'd get to my feet, all nightmares shed,
and smile at danger past.

Josep Carner

Josep Llimona

Gnarled and powerful and ruddy like you see him,
this giant who seems like some great hulking
Russian peasant revolutionary,
going forward all the while looking for fight,
this man smelling of clay and wheat,
impressive like some clumsily baked archangel,
bears, with an immortal's body — gentling, gripping —
the fires of heaven, clods of earth.

Josep Llimona (1864-1934), well-known Catalan sculptor.

Josep Carner

Palace Sweepers' Song

The great palace would be shamed, if we at daybreak failed
    to come with sweeping brushes.
We clean away, each time, a night's offences,
    lest the dawn complain.

    Folly's leavings we thresh apart;
our slavery's avenged by
auguries of drooping feathers,
withered flowers and broken glass.

Rolling the carpets back and scrubbing the stone floors,
    opening doors and windows wide,
a stench of things abominable startles —
    in corners and on thrones alike.

    The dust we raise will turn to sparks,
for it carries news of malefaction, fraud.
Let those who never crossed a palace threshold
keep that well in mind on the day of wrath.

Josep Carner

Come Late to Her Own Delight

Malice and blame, stay back.
Let her go on her way unnoticed,
her brow faded but she still rosy like childhood,
coming so late, now, to her own delight.

Her frail youth futile
(rose half-concealed in chervil and mallow),
quietly, now, her uneven tread
bears, hesitant, a full heart.

Servant of your dream, so gently stooping,
your humble kiss would appear sacred,
and the seven white strands in your hair can lead into languor
Love's insolent brow.

Josep Carner

Absence

No need for closing eyelids.
What's far is now made present.
I can see my house. The quietest
window unfolding,

slowly, in the shade;
the curtain barely sighs,
the glass gleams gently,
an autumn rose is weeping.

So much silence commends to me
a thought of most delicate cold;
I'd rather not open the blind
closed upon my garden.

For like one who's passed already
out of life, and can't believe it,
and goes smiling to the mirror and,
confronting it, sees no one there,

even if love drew near to me,
as to anticipate my will,
spirit alone might wait upon it;
never in those eyes could startle
any sigh or glance of mine.

Josep Carner

To a Toad

Rejected creature, scurry away from kicks;
with self-disgust your eyelids blink and burn;
the rays of sunlight, wonder and joy to others,
    for you are darts of scorn.

But then the night comes down, which deals gently
with ugliness, connecting, among the dreams bewitching
the roads — glum spittle of Satan —
smiling and hope in the mean hearts,
turning the plaintive cry into a loveliness
    unique and numberless.

In daytime people could kill you: they find you frightening;
but now you comfort the traveller, soothe his fright;
you may, who knows, even grow handsome when you sing,
    feeling secure, shutting your eyes tight.

Serene your song comes forth, compassionate counsel.
When music sounds from the heart, nothing torments.
And you, in the darkness, grow full of grace,
like a sunflower in the sun, like rain on grass.

Josep Carner

Company

Like a tyrant slanting to his ruin,
I grow each year that passes more alone;
death growls around the basement of my palace;
and all my flatterers are now reduced to four.

Until the night sinks down, all four stay with me,
moving swarms of light thoughts about;
they are my fine-voiced intimates, they give
disillusion a cradle, dreams to the heart.

When everyone is sleeping they draw still closer,
can suit their measure to my desire;
they hide, from these eyes, all other things,

wishful that my delight be not disturbed.
The lamp, a book, a rose, are they,
and a great tree blacker than the night.

Josep Carner

Death of a Squirrel

Evening came, now more gold than blue.
A squirrel crouched in the fork
of a thorn-tree, on the path leading
to the pine-wood — that coil of tail
heavy, now, upon his back;
his head grew slack, his foot in agony
made a branch move.

He wanted, left with only one sad stain
of hair on brown, furrowed skin,
to make an end; his dulled sight hid
the green road of leaves he'd gone so fast along;
his final waning instinct felt
summer shutting, life stopping,
and fear retreating never to return.

I walked across the grass on tiptoe.
Bees crowded the heather.
Nearing the city cleaved by swallows,
thrushes filled an elder-tree.
And I, mortal, my leisure spoilt,
in my shadow, at my side, saw
how stooped I was beneath the weight of sorrow.

Josep Carner

Sunday Sea

Velvet and silver, enchantingly smooth,
a Sunday sea, in her glad rags,
anointed with oils of peace,
all pleated, print.

No restless wind, within
the pleasant circle, stirs.
For the sea hears Mass in recollected mood
in this lost fishing port.

A big Saint Peter in the little church
from so much smell of seaweed breathes new life.
Jesus preaches in a boat. A seagull flies
around the pointed bell tower.

The altar's empty, now Mass is over.
Compunction filling her bright gaze,
the sea still hopes a mother mourning
her drowned son may come
today, being filled with heaven, to forgive the sea.

Josep Carner

Island

Crag above dancing roads,
island, sudden solitude, prodigy, sea-
tower gazing at fugitive
boats and clouds — oh not that you lack
or ever can stop the days' encroachment. Breakers
drive clefts in your caves. An arm of sea
sweeps close in to Cap-a-la-Terra,
your pine trees come unkempt, fearing
the sea-depths howling on the move.

You and I erect! And though we happen
to play, at times, foreigners with each other
(the custom being that even love sunders),
you and I together! Since I was born
you watched over my breath; for me you invented
shapes and colours, to give me a chance to live.
And watching me open my eyes each morning
gives you the courage to go on living.
Had I no mornings, who'd re-make you?

Spells of yours fill my senses:
dust-clad, foam-grassed wind,
the sky with its flock circling around in it,
old Proteus, music-maker of change,
life itself, that pointless urgent breathing,
mad delight spreading throughout the blood
from only a brilliance of appearances;
and virtue everywhere unaided,
testing space by the angle of its wings.

All things are signs, and no signs last.
What can you hope to do, red crag,

in the common claws of change,
even if that rock-pose of yours were true,
and the steep slopes, all that abruptness, real,
even if you were not an imaginary island,
made, re-made, inhabited in dreams,
built of memory and the impossible,
only against my spirit to be measured?

Island three times over: one of your circles spreads
a great way off, it summons me and does not answer;
another is a retinue of shadows;
and one, closer to hand, is made of mist and plaint.
And now, at the centre of an unfamiliar
inlet — core of an arc protecting me and
surrendering me — these eyes forget the earth,
and the surf slips through my fingers,
and I'm homesick for all things that flow gently in light.

Let the sun when it goes down before me
still find me ready to build myself a small
fire — soft eye of dark,
last gloaming task. When, island,
shall we know the irrevocable sleep?
If you, inert no longer,
could be rowed like a boat through darkness,
leaving no wake in the silence,
the mast warped, the sails alive . . .

Josep Carner

An Old Man Returns

Coming back with hope
flying at the masthead, the ship advances:
delight, at the prow, is like an instinct.
Yet an old man at the stern says, wrapping himself up
against who knows what shiverings to come:
'Often what you find is
the cities sleeping and the hearts drenched with absence;
even in the place that once was yours,
you pass by, and are not seen, you look and are not there.'

JOSEP CARNER

At Nightfall

It's late. Roads don't tempt me now.
And from the closed-in garden I can tell
the days and leaves and flowers
are fallen, trampled in the mist.

My steps turn furtive
like a hesitant foreigner's.
Dahlia spectres
sigh in a tearful dark.

Far away, a bell sound floats,
joining the living to the dead.
Invincible, the night spreads out,
a sea of desert islands.

The lamp on the table summons me,
so does a fleeting thought,
and the old worn chair,
and, malcontent, a sheet of paper.

Josep Carner

Farewells

Great walnut-tree baroque,
maternal branches like a hen's wings:
already boys are pouring over their books,
and a squirrel reaches up to the last lone fruit.

The land is plundered, has nothing to offer;
you can hear a snow warning deep in air.
Scutters of leaves run hunted down the road,
and overhead the clouds are edged with grey.

Triumphant in the fearless pine trees,
a rook's grating cry
proclaims today the opaque weather
of small fires and crouched lives.

Josep Carner

Belgium

If foreign lands were meant for me
I'd like to grow old in a country
where the light filtered, smiling, yellow and grey;
where streams are the eyes of meadows
marked out by trees of whitethorn, elm, and pear;
to live quietly, never pointed out,
among a nation of good, united people,
heart side by side with heart, city by city;
and high-roads and lamplight
advancing through the fields.
Sky and cloud, cruel or kind,
would captive rest in canals of trembling water
that wanted nothing save to mirror stars.

I'd like to grow old in a city
where the soldiers are not too soldierly,
where everyone grows tender about music and painting,
or, when in flower, the cherry of Japan;
where neither child nor workman needs compassion,
where you can see interiors of houses full
of talking and pipe-smoke and hospitality,
and flowers of burning colours:
splendid surprise right through the coldest weather.
And quite often, at the very doors of a church,
a famous, colourful marketplace would sprout
the sea's booty, the earth's bounty,
and plenty of each for all.

A city for walking round, for searching out —
in melancholy's name, or seeking novelty,
chinking clear and sharp —
old houses in whose grounds the shadows nest,

and many newer ones, with small front gardens.
Wise men could there be found, of many kinds;
and a hundred eminent umbrellas
would make — in use, alas — official ranks
at the unveiling of monuments.
And certain long walks would suddenly end
in beech-woods, in park-ponds, in clearings
designed for love, delight, solitude, tears.

By much forsaken, from much abstaining,
I would live in others, a little in each.
But none
should fear that little, as they made their way.
One might, by chance, frequent an ancient garden,
good for resting in, with a glittering fountain
and goldfish, that make for gaiety.
Of me the children, with their bits of bread, might say:
'That's the man who comes here every day.'

Josep Sebastià Pons (1886-1962)

Her Arm was so Bright

Her arm was so bright when, smiling,
she brought us water, salt, bread,
all we could think of was snow.
Her walk was a natural dance.

In her blood were Greece and Conflent,
in her face the wind kindled
a thousand roses
as down the wood she went.

Joan Salvat-Papasseit (1894-1924)

Christmas

I feel the cold of the night
                     and the dark beat of the drum:
and the group of young men passing by singing.
I hear the celery cart
                 clattering the pavement
and its rivals beating it to the marketplace.

The women in the kitchen,
                    beside the burning stove,
have turned the gaslight up and plucked the chicken.
Now when I look at the moon it seems to be at the full;
impatient for tomorrow,
                   they gather up the feathers.

Tomorrow round the table we'll forget the poor —
and how poor we are ourselves.
                    Jesus newly born
will look at us for a minute over the dessert,
and having looked
              burst into tears.

Joan Salvat-Papasseit

Long Live Love

Long live the love   my girl gave me
fresh and clean like a May-time bliss!
Long live love
               I called her and she came —
she was all white like a surge of milk.

Long live the love   she too delighted in:

Long live the love
                    I wanted and I took.

PERE QUART (1899-1986)

Holidays with Pay

I've made up my mind to go away for ever.
Amen.

I'll come back tomorrow
because I'm old
and my feet are spoilt,
swollen with gout.

But I'll be back the day after,
made young by disgust.
For ever and ever. Amen.

And the day after that I'll come back,
like a carrier pigeon,
stupid as him,
but not so straight,
not even white either.

Poisoned by myths,
creels crammed with blasphemies,
bony, shrunk, bleared,
a prince dispossessed even of his dream,
fake Job;
tongue-cut, gelt,
grazing for lice.

I'll take the train to those holidays with pay.
Clinging to the buffers.
The land that was once our inheritance
runs away from me.
A gush between my legs
rejecting me.

Grass, rock:
pledges of love dissolving in shame.
Oh skyless land!

But look at me now:
I'm back again.
All alone, so leprous I'm nearly blind.
I'm off tomorrow —
and this time I mean it.
Yes yes, I'm away on all fours,
like great-great-grandad,
by the smugglers' short cut
to the black frontier of death.

Then I'll leap into the burning darkness
where all is foreign.
Where the ancient god of my fathers
lives, in exile.

PERE QUART

Litany

For the children
> lies.
For the lovers
> lies.
For friends
> lies.
For the customers
> lies.

Lies plump or lean,
firm or tender — kisses, vows;
living — as fresh blood;
wise, grateful.
Fraud, fib.
Half-lies.

And historical lies
which now we can pin on our lying grandfathers.
Literary lies —
two lies per line.
Metaphysical lies —
time, and being, God damn them!
Lies technical, and scientific:
figures that become machines
and machines that lie
like mad legends.

And the lies of faith
that make up the sad great misericordia
heaven has for the suffering
and wretched of the earth;
high fabulous lies

that one day, I don't know how,
somebody says turn certainties.
(Thanks, Lord, in advance,
credit without security,
as if it *were* that way.
Amen, Amen, O Lord!
Can you hear this cry, O Lord?)

For death, when it kills us, lies!

Pere Quart

The Nurse

There was a nurse
all white and gold
with an angel-face of the best they've painted.
She smiled discreetly, almost severely,
as she walked down the street beneath the acacias
into April;
she looked at the sky from blue pupils.

Her friend beside her, half a step behind her,
pressed her arm
cautiously, greedily.

The red-haired virgin went her way
towards her work that would not wait,
winged and tense, gently eluding
the imploring words
of the brown, dishevelled youth
who wanted to brake her and hold her back
and make her understand, here and now,
that he and she were everything:
water and thirst, the earth,
fire and grain,
the sacred breath of the dead,
the new life,
the heart's blood
and the always travelling folly
of the only fecund sin.

'Let's love each other, Adela!'

But the girl was a nurse
and she was late.

146 Heavily entangled
in a stale duty
she nearly flew, all out of breath,
towards her job,
stolid puppy, vain little machine.

Pere Quart

Vixen

What can we make from the skin
of a lady of fashion?
Coats for our Sister Vixen.

PERE QUART

Children

Life at dust-level, gaze-high;
warm silk of snow and mud fresh on their cheeks.

Hope and envy — hawk-bells of the heart;
faithless like time, sudden as luck

(or death); miserable and playful: children,
cheating and secret, or prodigal as sultans;

in the sun's glare, garden terrorists,
frightened in the desert of night; impassive killers

of dragonflies and roses; peddlers of flattery,
addicts of tenderness, milk-drunkards.

The furtive pleasure of splash and mire,
in blood the unguessed promise of love —

storm-disguises, pain's adornment,
pity's painting, tide of fear,

their tears determined, sonorous, lavish,
weapons in their civil war against the giants.

PERE QUART

The Date

I won't stop, and you keep walking:
as though we didn't know each other.
The city's confused voices, difficult signals,
trouble me; through eyes of others
and in mirrors,
death finds me out
and asks me questions.
Now keep on walking.

At the other side of the line
the path to be taken leads down.
Then you come to a turn.
When you cross the stone bridge
keep straight on up.
Don't turn to the left
until you get to the field
planted with living cypress trees
and dead crosses.

I may get there before you;
if not, wait for me.
And don't sit down, stay standing,
entire and vertical, not like the rest of them.
And still moist, like a tree.

What we need is a high sky,
a noon dishevelled
by the wind of great journeys.
Night is too pious: it cloys.
And with all those stars, it deludes.

Life is only a fashion, woman, *you* know that already.
As from today, the hidden shape
of nakedness must assert itself
towards the line of bone
until the first and final dust.

Disappointed, unprepared,
let's say goodbye and forget ourselves
with null, marmoreal gestures.
Gravity's infallible.

Yet — who knows? — they might, at the eleventh hour,
plant wings upon us.
I never claimed to understand any mystery.
Tricked out in law supreme, I stay ignorant,
in mortal wisdom — and in avarice.

And now, walk.

Pere Quart

Game

I navigate against the current.
When the rest are coming back I'm setting out.

Before taking thought I think it over.
I weep and smile in silence
and alone

I seek the ring I lost
in a region of light and well-being.

*Tutto ch'altrui aggrada me disgrada.**

When I can I differ.
For example:
I don't say 'prickly pear'
but *'opuntia'*.
And to lose a living
I work on Sundays.

Moribund I'll celebrate —
should the family permit,
and the other powers —
my birth.

*The first line of a sonnet by the Italian poet, Cino da Pistoia
(1270-1337). It means: Everything other people like, I dislike.

PERE QUART

Christmas Card

They plant a tree without roots
in the living-room
and make it sprout, of a sudden, with
torró from Fatjó's
and an electric train.
The favoured one,
the sweet monopolist,
can reach down a star —
just like that — if he wants,
for the squalling infant
who's dirtied himself.

So you see:
working miracles isn't a thing for saints
any longer.

Nor does anyone feel surprised —
not even the rancid virgin,
refined sacristy-arse —
if the Babe goes naked
winter and night.

For three-toned Christmas cards
the poor get into debt.

And using for pretext the King of Kings
we'll behead as many Innocents as need be.

No, I am not exaggerating.

Torró (Catalan), *turrón* (Castilian), a sweet similar to nougat
or almond-paste.

Pere Quart

Country

At night, the kiss: a furtive grazing.
Looking is useless. But the hands
move apart like two brothers
setting off to seek their fortunes.

Hill, valley, trembling grass!
The air breathes better than ever there
when earthquake beaches on
the softest isle, the best-loved space.

PERE QUART

Final Night

A black sea, tavern and bed
for abominable stars.
Nights are not for angels.

Give us back paradise.
Look at our broad palms,
our teeth devoid of enamel.

Blood and seed. Dry fountain.
Tears of rainwater.
Look at our big ears.

The gloom stinks,
and mothers, hammer in hand,
watch over earthenware babes.

The three angels of night
are playing cards,
and losing their wings,
at the sign of the dolphins.

Blind laughter. Black
sea-scum. Final night.
The moon waned
so much it died.

Bartomeu Rosselló-Porcèl (1913-1938)

'A single sidewalk tree brings in . . .'

A single sidewalk tree brings in
the sea's tremor, the leaves chafing together
create again the kindness of waves.
Dead rocks on dead sands
survive in a few tufts of frightened grass.
Mad sea of grey and green, vast air:
smash glass on the bland coast!
Decipher the distant shadow, blue and white,
of clouds replete with wind, prodigal of wings.
Only in me can you grow, and spread
a purer salt, more hidden stone,
yet find yourself again on roads made dark
by distant whales and ancient seaweed.
But I am lost on the wide plains
of oak and evergreen,
where dancing has been forgotten, and the cry of water,
and the moon sees no rivers,
or wells, or tall waves.

SALVADOR ESPRIU (1913-1985)

from *The Bull-skin*

1

The bull, in the Sepharad ring,
attacked the stretched skin
and, tossing it high,
made it a flag.
Against the wind, that blood-covered
bull-skin is turned a rag
the gold of the sun has thickened,
forever given over to the martyrdom
of time, our prayer
and blasphemy.
At once victim and executioner,
hatred, love, lament, laughter,
under a closed eternity of sky.

2

A spread bull-skin,
that's you, old Sepharad.
The sun can't dry,
bull-skin,
the blood we all have spilt,
or shall spill tomorrow,
bull-skin.
If I gaze across the sea,
or lose myself deep in song
or far inside the dream,
whenever I dare to look
at my heart and its dread,

I see that spread bull-skin,
old Sepharad.

3

The skin's a drum
beaten by hands
of fear,
by a galloping horse
which cannot win
the final prize
of rest.
Death and Sepharad,
lean horse and mad,
you cannot often
tell their names apart
in the grievous
dream of time.

4

Lean horse galloping
sad years along the rough
roads of Sepharad.

Dry grief demands
kind water, and wheat.
Lest what bright rain we have
turn blood.

Our night, the attentive
ear of dread,

can hear approaching,
across the broad bull-skin,
a lipless laughter,
nightmare mounted.

5

If you run all the time
through the night of your hatred,
mad horse of Sepharad,
the whip and the sword
must govern you.
Who spills blood
cannot elect a prince,
nor can one who betrays, robs,
or neglects to build,
slowly, the temple
of his work.
In the first fire you burn
freedom.

Approach and observe
yourself in this glass,
learn the true
name of your ill:
in the face of the idol
see yourself.

6

An idol you raised, in the likeness of your ills.

On a far-off day of our winter,
still under the protection of this sky,
at the heart of envy we saw with dread
the great crime of Sepharad take root:
the sin so unendingly sad
of triumphless war between brothers.
Come from across the sea to these
barren lands forever drenched in blood,
we took refuge in the pain of work,
found our way by the light of the remembered temple,
and won, slowly, a free peace.

7

Our forebears watched,
many years back,
that self-same sky
of winter, high and sad,
reading a strange token
of help and rest therein.
And the oldest wanderer
showed it to the others,
pointing authority's
long staff,
indicating, then, these fields,
and said:
'Surely we can rest here
from the vast journeyings
of the Golah.

Surely it's here
you'll bury me.'

And so they were,
all of them, buried
one by one in Sepharad,
all those who came with him,
and their children and grandchildren,
right down to ourselves.
For we know well enough that many of us
are still scattered
in the wind, in the wandering,
of the Golah.
But we don't want to lament
the temple any more,
nor suffer the endless yearning
for that city of ours.

That's why, when someone
from time to time comes up to us,
and with a stern look
enquires:
'Why stay here, in this
rough, dry country,
so full of blood?
Surely this can't be
the best land you could find
in all the ample
time of trial
in the Golah,'
we, with a light smile
accorded by the memory
of parents and forebears,

answer only:
'In our dream, it is.'

    8

Don't lament, any more,
the temple destroyed.
Open sea-roads
await you in the west.

Canticles, like royal archers,
will no longer be intoned
on the high wall: but be
saved in memory.

By gazing we brought
that city sky with us.
In our eyes dark reasons
learn clear dreams.

Beggars descended
from lords, dispersed
by millennial winds,
we've come to Sepharad.

And how we love this new
land whose bitter bread always
leaves on our old mouths
an aftertaste of blood!

9

They sow dryness
in earth drenched
in blood alone.

By tired hands
aroused to the furrows —
the first flight of
the birds of dawn.

Sepharad steeps
in a great thirst for water
great hunger for bread.

10

If buying bread you're given
tinted chalk,
your teeth, nibbling,
must break;
your pain make smile
the man who knows
the whereabouts of lime
and flour.
So you fall into
a decline, fattening
the robber who sold
false goods.

The servant takes the air
astride the horse
of the prince who now

goes barefoot.
With a noose he measures
head and shoulders
of the master who lost
(but made no sound)
the very last
vestige of dignity.
How can you bear it, Lord?
And won't the packman think
it's high time
to get down?

Dangerous to think —
cheap deaf delusion —
the complex, anxious
truth
of the sick old man,
covered in quilts and blankets
drenched in blood guilt shed,
has stopped beating.
Listen to the voice of ice
talking to you,
hope in captivity,
feeble tick-tock:
the clock's last heart
never stops.

11

On a slow beat, the heart of time
travels, bearing us deeper into
pronouns' narrow deceit.
We are sometimes you,

almost never him but always I,
whenever, unremitting,
they force me to repeat
jail's first word.
We pass, joined only by the bridge
in that gaze of chill dread,
by staring, empty eyes,
one by one through Nothing;
while out of order goes
night's final tap,
and not one drop of water falls
to the dry lips of Sepharad.

14

We know some kept, in high
strange attics ruled
by thick webs and cold,
an ancient copper brazier lacking one leg,
a tripod brazier, lame now
and covered in verdigris;
and what we'd like is for someone, some day, to use it,
little by little, but unremitting, to warm
Sepharad's adverse winter.
But now for the rice over a slow fire chirp,
in front of the open mouths of children's hunger,
the scant fish we caught
in the drenching hazard of the sea.
The fish are three, the brazier tripod, each
and all we designate by the names —
in a clear, diminutive hand inscribed —
of justice, honesty, and work.
And we ask the gaping young to dine,

show them, insistently, the meagre meal
to calm their need a little,
enabling them, after, with chilled fingers, to light,
having let in the light and the air to these forgotten garrets,
the first and everlasting coals in the tripod brazier.

21

Mills of Sepharad:
little by little
dreams will grow real.

Wind-mill, blood-mill:
you must grind even the bones
if we are to have good bread.

By words we descend
the deep well of panic:
then by fragile phrases climb
to a new clarity.

25

Let us tell the truth, unremittingly,
for the honour of serving, under the feet of all men.

Let us loathe big bellies, and big words,
the indecent facades of money,
the badly dealt cards of luck,
thick smoke of incense burning towards the powerful.
Vile now is the nation of grandees,
it squats in its own hatred like a dog,

barks from afar, at hand accepts the stick,
and beyond the clay traverses roads of death.

With song we build in darkness
high walls of dreaming, under cover of this tempest.
Across the night come sounds of many fountains:
let us close the doors on fear.

26

I keep in the darkness
the door well closed
and dogs alert against
the fear of thieves.
The silkworm wind eats on,
its mouth is never still.

Leaves of dreams we had
one by one are eaten up.
Nostalgia gnawed away
most painfully.
O Sepharad, our son,
tree of bare boughs.

A long silk thread it makes
to be our winding-sheet.
But weavers' hands prefer
warmth made of wool.
Great pain kept silent must
a free cry beget.
We'll dress up this last love
in hope.

Awake within the heart
of time, I guard the house.
To the approaching light
I'll give the key: the night,
well-walked, becomes,
step by step, the dawn.

35

White birds, overhead, are flying south,
in the spacious light of this long day,
the roads of good weather, one by one, come to an end,
the last doors to freedom close.
And now the fleshless hand strikes the tambourine,
thin lips are telling us 'haviv',
with horrifying love, while our tired limbs
go on dancing, dancing unendingly,
and we laugh and make others laugh till the tears come,
in the most extreme disquiet of joy.
There's a breath of wind in cypress, fennel and vine,
the sea remains, and the wings have opened
a greater clarity for us, awakened more desire
for a sky merciful and great, new Sepharad sky.

36

Led by the nose,
we sped to the beach:
pirouetting
with Nicholas the bear.

haviv: Hebrew for love.

Cheats and thieves —
in Sepharad, kings —
joined us in jumping
and frolics,
and caned us on head
and shoulders.
From high Sinera's
bell-tower, Death,
watching us, cried out
how much it loved me.
Fleshless hands
beat time, and laughter shook
this live enclosure.
You can't say that I
ate off someone else,
for sweating out the dance
I always paid,
from soup to sweet,
for hunger's meal.
Black cloud
that suddenly hid
the day's brightness
will take away
the dry fields'
poor crop.
Swallows flying
near the rushes,
and the grapes, at sea-
level, ripening.

37

The grapes grew ripe, and all of a sudden the spread
slow summer rose before us,
like a wall, imposing
on inward sight a strange return;
we gazed, on our way, at lost clarities.
Here you have the sea, the trees and vineyards,
and even ourselves, beneath a Sepharad sky.
We'll give each thing a final name, when old
memories make, almost, a new creation.
You know quite well there's nothing after — except
the quiet, cold, solitary, dark light,
rungs and wells of light, where
words quenched, vanished on silence-back.
Deep down, a sound of galloping
over long night roads of blackest water;
we feel that fear is where we're best invented.

42

Let those young hands —
clean, strong, and cold —
learn to count.

You'll fall heir to
days of hatred
and misgovernment.

Watch, alert,
where the money-pot
lies hidden.

If you want power,
see that it's yours
before giving orders.

By ropes of light we came
down the abyss
of lost dreams.

Gently the boats
moved off to their wrecking
on high seas far away.

By smoke-ladders
blind eyes climbed
the cliffs.

A flower's brief life:
hope ill at ease, and the slow
weevil at his work.

Thirst grew calmer:
hell laughed
at charity.

The prince of the world
sat us at table,
to dine with Death.

We devoured pork
and cuts off other
honourable pigs.

Then, well fattened up,
were suddenly whisked
from chair to plate.

The teeth reached
to the marrowbone
of great thoughts.

The molars crunch
the arc of a spine
that curved so much.

Take heart. Is it only
a little air
the wind bears off?

You ask, and the words
are stones cast
from weird slings.

They round upon you till
you're crushed as though beneath
massive ruined castles.

By dirt-paths
we led diversity
towards unity.

And the effort left us
with neither flock
nor shepherd.

We can't understand why
we cover up the void
of nothingness in words.

From the quiver of time
we drew the arrow
of our lamentation.

And plunged a cry
like a knife in the hard
heart of Sepharad.

44

Blue against
the sun:
this trunk
of a dead tree.
Over the burning
stubble, a wide-
sweeping
falcon-flight.
In the furrows
no ripeness,
in the pepper-trees
no sound of any
fresh wind.
In song
no solace,
no rest.
At the heart
of harvest,
slow flocks

in a long dust.
To the fear
which I am,
which all of us are,
memory alone
can open up —
in dry wells,
in a hankering after
the old ice
of fountains —
the never-again
road back.

51

We grasped, in wandering,
the trees' grown serenity,
against the great night-threshold wind.
We loved the earth
and our own dream of a new house
built on freedom's land.
No sure flower, but surely hope
in a sure flower plucked and brought
along with all this pilgrim dust.
Abandoning words, we feel now
arrived at silence by the sound
of riders in the distance.

52

In the silence
ringed by sound,

bull-skin spread out
for all to tread.
When those young fingers
raise it from the dust,
quiver it high
above the resting
ones who loved it
as bloodstained rag:
we who served it
in days of grief.

The far procession
is now near.
First to approach,
a cantering horse.
A lipless rider
laughs our name.
The cold word
we hear unfrightened,
for in hope we save
the last and naked
heart of every thing,
of man, the well
where hate takes root,
and all the enormous pain
of an old ill
forgiving waters drown.

54

We want only,
hoping
yet humble,

the eternal fullness
of the rose,
a supreme eternity
in flower.

While the houses of night
close one by one,
and the dark withdraws
to the source of dawn,
from hypersensitive
blind fingers
our eyes learn
to look, to know,
to understand
with slow love.

So we have travelled
the rivers and mountains,
the high plateau and the cities,
and we sleep every dream
their men have.
We have been with the wind
in the fields, in the woods,
in the sound of leaves and fountains,
and little by little we are writing
on this furtive, immortal heart,
on stretched skin,
the name
of Sepharad.

Salvador Espriu

La Main Gauche

While I burn out, perishing
of the woods' vast thirst,
poor relations consuming
all my bread predict
rainfall over the sea's
calmness; covered in the derision
that spills from glutted bellies,
I'm now the friend of unjust
riches; and, exhausted,
mere ash, I wait,
defenceless against the hurt
of the final answer, simply
for the cruel laughter
of the people of my own blood,
when they reside forever
in the places of light,
to become, in immobile time,
the solace, and the sole delight of
my darkness.

SALVADOR ESPRIU

Dance of Death

Through all the various chances
of our time, the subtle
rain must reunite us,
and, within the listening night,
the rebel wax of slow
tapers burn, an army
agonized by the distant
order of the serene
homelands of light, the noble
silence-bearers.

Salvador Espriu

Song of Tiresias

Death, to look at you,
has robbed me of eyes.

Lost, I clamour and, blinded,
beg. Death stares.

You hide beyond your mountains,
where you call yourself safe.

Perhaps you think: 'I have dogs,
I keep money, I know books.

Can the diviner recognize me —
so deep in these dreams?'

Yes, very like the others:
face, road, shelter.

But Death took some old
eyes, and approached.

Salvador Espriu

Diptychs of the Living

Perhaps a line will save me from the sea,
a few clear words:
if, that is, they can stretch their value
over an entire life.
But I fear those words may prove
so little value that I beseech
the beggars' hunger
for the humblest alms:
pray for me, for the captives'
dream, for our
suffering, for those who carry
both on lips and in heart
the sign of dust,
and of death.

Salvador Espriu

Attempted Canticle in the Temple

How tired I am of this,
my craven, ancient, savage fatherland;
how it would delight me to leave and go
beyond the farthest north,
where the people, they say, are noble and clean,
cultured, rich, and free,
unsupervised and happy!
But then my disapproving brethren would tell
    the congregation:
'Leaving his native place a man becomes
like a bird leaving the nest,'
while I, in the distance, laughed
at the law, the antique wisdom,
of this my arid people.
But the dream will never be followed,
I'll stay here till my death.
For I too am full of cowardice and savagery,
and also in despair and pain love this poor land,
my sad, unclean, unlucky fatherland.

Salvador Espriu

Felt in the Manner of Salvador Espriu

The time has come to pay my old price, death;
already these eyes are weary of the light.
My deprivations have descended all the steps,
and now I'm driven deeper into night's dominion.

I become in silence king of the night,
and know myself a servant of men who suffer.
But how can I direct this enormous suffering
toward the words of night in their paddock?

Winds and victory and repose pass
in a sequence of tall flames and archery.
Imprisoned in my name and in my dead ones,
I, travelled by me, become a wall.

And lose myself, and, missionless, am alone,
beyond singing, amid forgotten men
who died frightened: a mere dark dream
of one who came from places of light.

Vicent Andrés Estellés (1924-1993)

from *The Lover*

I respected, in you, all women;
I loved, in you, all life;
intensely, I kissed your ankle.
I wanted to be like an old-time lover.
Naked on the rumpled bed
you lay, spreadeagled:
in your ankle I kissed existence,
love, sorrow, pleasure, and toil.

BLAI BONET (1926-1997)

Conversation

Conversing, someone said:
'Just as the oats were dying,
hands of love bound them,
unbound them, and they lived.'

And the more they discussed it,
the more silver branches, the more
sounds of gleaming oats
came and went.
By the dint of words
spoken on land, in the air,
on the four sea ways,
the hour, the fresh hour
of the first dawn
of rivers, of aviaries,
is always vast and always now.
If we talk, we comment
on the multiple clarity
of the mouth and hands
of God, who talks, and is
possessor of the word.
And that time-honoured talk
is as tender a success
in warm mouths
as a shiver of green
above a black tree-trunk.

BLAI BONET

Inner Night

If clarity is heard
in such young calm,
it comes from one thing only:
having taken, at night,
between silent hedges, the dark
road of compliant ignorance.

To walk through a dark land implies
a deep desire to shine.

To say yes to every minute,
every air and water,
is not to exaggerate a gesture
for the purpose of conferring
sun, oranges,
bright rivers or hands of love.

To say yes to every air implies
the will to take
what you neither know nor feel,
and wait, naked of gesture,
for fruit that no one promised you;
and believe, like a fountain,
that you give clarity, and shine,
but are blind and noisy.

With such equipment, lover,
the lines of your hand full
of solitude, over the curious
strand of astounded senses,
walk, leap, fly, quickly,

cross hearing the sound
of your own unique and bright
wheatstalk Spring.

BLAI BONET

The Word

It's enough to say a word —
'plantain' or 'curlykale' —
and the world sounds clearer
than in branch-clarities.
What a washed clarity
has the world in its mouth!

What an ancient tremor to
name 'garlic', and feel
the luminous distance
between the colour of a stalk
and its name sounding in me!

The word is the world
rising anointed from God's
deep constant dawn
in us, pallid lovers.
And we are human reeds
whom God plays, when we talk.
Fragile reeds,
but full of music.

MIQUEL MARTÍ I POL (1929-)

For All of Us

If we sing dumb, who'll speak out?
Our words don't carry much weight.
We've precious little clout, we're too
frivolous to make them listen.
All the same, whatever
is most pure in us
is worth as much — and well we know it —
as all the unease felt by any scion of
this long distinguished line of the defeated.
We must insist,
like beggars if you will,
at a hundred barred doors.

Miquel Martí i Pol

In Memoriam

He believed in marvels until a timely
hole in his right lung dried up his heart
like a root left out in the sun.
He was about nineteen and tenderness
stained his skin like an eczema.

He suffered little. When death surprised him
he uttered a few curses in a clear voice
and spat blood, solemn and unashamed.

Now he rests in peace.
Let us pray for him.

Francesc Vallverdú (1935-)

Our Humanity

When we no longer leave everything to the political
boyos, and when we've stripped them of all their mythical
haloes, and the way we say 'All men are equal' is truly
   emphatic,
and nobody finds that false but it's taken for axiomatic;
when we settle all disputes while sitting round a table
and, accepting words, make blows unacceptable;
when, if a madman rules us, all men meet,
firmly, to put him inside inside of a week;
when everyone really loves his neighbour as himself, although
he's African or Chinese, Algerian or Eskimo —
it's then we'll have achieved the grace we seek:
of making democracy real, and human beings complete.

FRANCESC VALLVERDÚ

Coffee and Cigars

'So, gentlemen, it's as I say: there's nothing on earth to match
good bourgeois good taste.
If something annoys us — why, we just make it taboo
as a warning to the young (that being the surest method
of shutting people up, while saving their face),
and then it can't upset us any more, or get under our skin.
Please! No sex, if you don't mind: love is prettier.
Unruly love, you say? For goodness' sake, my dear man,
was ever a love seen that was not sanctified?
Rub it out (that's better) and put "sin" instead.
Hunger? How do you spell it? With a haitch as in happiness?
Well, I myself recall having to eat at six once, I was that
    famished.
Admittedly herrings or dry bread is no one's idea of bliss,
but who would say no to it either?
What, money? Always the same old story! You'd think there
    was nothing
else in the world — as if Art, and Poetry, did not exist?
Oh leave me alone, please, I'm weary of cudgelling my brains —
and facts are facts, it's getting late, it's time to dine.'

Joan Margarit (1938-)

from *An Old Misunderstanding*

When Cavafy didn't even cut the pages
of the book that I inscribed to him with such
devotion, I remembered we are wells of scorn
and should not seek behind the words a face
as bright as our own dreams.
So I forgot the poets, but the poems
I made as much my own as cypress-shadow
or the bright sky in the window. That's what ran
through the mind of Kariotakis when Cavafy
didn't even cut the pages of the book
that he'd inscribed to him with such devotion.

Joan Margarit

Water

We can speak of water or the girl
since the girl and water
come together in my memory.
The girl is water: is freedom
for a shoulder that, under the skin,
has the palpable stiffness of an anchor.
The tenderness of water rescued
her so frail legs: I see again
blue swimming pools heated
to the temperature of her heart,
so far away in those remembered winters.
Pools her memory swims in.
I'm left with the iron sea at S'Aucanada —
all those white shells, jewels lost
among pebble-lights in water.
And the final sea — wind-tossed — sunglasses
covering the reddened eyes, which say:
water that was her freedom is now
the mirror restoring her to us.

Francesc Parcerisas (1944-)

Fragments

A girl playing the violin.
Umberto Saba's cat.
Cypress-tree shadows in Fiesole.
The window of Galileo's house.
Drizzle on the marketplace of Arezzo.
Such a setting of mist and beauty
deep in the ravenous gaze.
The theatre is empty, there's no show tonight.
You're a spectator in a deserted house,
a stray dog taking shelter in a palace.

Francesc Parcerisas

The Defeated

Those who invade the streets, in their sheepskin coats,
their medals and their uniforms, are a different race.
                    — Felicidad Blanc, *Espejo de sombras*

What is gained in losing
                    — Robert Lowell

They are Franco's troops and they have won the battles.
For you there's nothing left but the grave or beyond,
the luckless marvel of waking up among the ashes.
You hear a shout: 'It's them! They're coming!'
and feel like cowards, afraid, offended.
You were done down by an abject shadow of life.
And now, fifty years later — too young
to look for reparation — I can still see you,
silent with a trembling finger at your lips,
and I love you submitting to an order of great fear,
with the dignity of being in the right
or under nocturnal headlights of defeat.
Your silence has been a tangled wire,
showing us what is gained in losing.

Àlex Susanna (1957-)

Hands

Caresses we give each other from time to time
just before falling asleep,
when outside only the wind is howling
and everything inside the house
is taking a rest from itself,
have more, perhaps, to say about our love
than all the eagerness we often
embrace each other with,
when driven by a storm of desire:
the selfsame wind could play
on softer, smoother places,
while these two hands,
cautious now and callused,
know only how to wander
where love is found.

ÀLEX SUSANNA

A Crowd of Faces

thinking of Lucian Freud

to Víctor Batallé

An evening train can seem
a museum of the horrors of tiredness,
these devastated faces
stitched with intestinal scars;
where are they coming from,
what homes heading for,
all so undone, so inert?
Some days disfigure us beyond healing:
how can we climb back to valour,
clutch on to words or whatever
so as to be once again
a human being who can think and feel?
Some days life covers us deep
in a dark cloak of defeat,
and by the time we sleep we've turned
into a shadow of flesh.

Translator's Acknowledgements

I nearly suggested putting, after my name on the title-page of this book, the phrase 'With a little help from my friends'. Or, better still, 'With a lot of help from my friends'. But I settled instead on a list, in alphabetical order, of those who have, in one way or another, helped me with these translations over the years, including some who are now dead. I hope I haven't forgotten anyone.

So here are the names, with all gratitude: Irene Alba Muñoz, Santiago Albertí, Emilio Araúxo Iglesias, Arlindo Barbeitos, Rosangela Barone, Allan Bell, Alan Biddle, Pól Breathnach, John Buckley, Melita Cataldi, Marie-Louise Colbert, Michael Cummins, Piero de Gennaro, David Devitt, Suwarsih Djodjo-poespito, Séamus Dooley, Salvador Espriu, David Ferrer, Joan Gili/Dolphin Books (publishers of *Josep Carner*, 1962), Seán Golden, Marisa González Feixóo, Louise Higham (British Council, Spain), Seán Hutton, Kate Ward Kavanagh, PJ Kavanagh, Mairéad Looby, Joe McArdle, Hugh McFadden, Liz McFadden, Albert Manent, Marià Manent, Kathleen March, Joan Margarit, Luis Martul, Joaquim Molas, Eiléan Ní Chuilleanáin, Máirín Ní Dhonnchadha, Pádraig Ó Conchuir, Cormac Ó Cuilleanáin, Michael O'Dea, Pádraig Ó Gormaile, Joan Oliver, Francesc Parcerisas, Ana Pinto, Daphne Ryan ('Sammy' Sheridan), Sebastian Ryan, Xosé Antón Serén, Michael Smith/New Writers' Press (publishers of *Friend Songs*, 1970), Marco Sonzogni, Àlex Susanna, Toni Turull, Francesc Vallverdú, Martin Veiga, Judith Willis, Macdara Woods, Vincent Woods, Suella Wynne.

And: I owe a special word of thanks to the publisher, Peter Fallon, for his encouragement and patience. After all, the whole thing was his idea in the first place.

Pearse Hutchinson

Acknowledgements

Pearse Hutchinson and The Gallery Press gratefully acknowledge permission to publish translations of copyright material by the following authors:

Manuel Altolaguirre: courtesy of Paloma Altolaguirre; **Mário António**: Carla Heloisa Oliveira and Ana Paula Oliveira. 'Noites de luar no morro da Maianga' from *100 Poemas* (1951); **Emilio Araúxo**: the author and Noitarenga. 'Nome' and 'Outubro' published in *As Chairas da Letra* (2000) © Editorial Noitarenga;

José Bergamín: Carmen Balcells Agency, Barcelona;

Josep Carner: Raimon Bergós/Bufet Bergós; **Luis Cernuda**: Ángel María Yanguas Cernuda;

Carlos Drummond de Andrade: Lucia Riff Literary Agency (Brazil);

Salvador Espriu: from *Obres completes* © Grup 62, Barcelona; **Vicent Andrés Estellés**: 'L'Amant' from *Cant Temporal* © Eliseu Climent, editor, © Hereus de Vicent Andrés Estellés / Editorial 3i4, València;

León Felipe: Alejandro Campos/León Felipe Foundation; **Celso Emilio Ferreiro**: from *Longa noite de pedra* © Herdeiros de Celso Emilio Ferreiro, 2003 © Edicións Xerais de Galicia, 2003;

Amedeo Giacomini: the author; **Lupe Gómez**: 'Falo e escrebo . . .' published in *Poesía fea* (2000) © Editorial Noitarenga;

Judith Herzberg: the author and De Harmonie Publishers, Amsterdam;

Joris Iven: the author, from *Egyptian Black* (1993);

Franco Loi: the author; **Arcadio López-Casanova**: the author;

Antonio Machado: José Rollán Riesco for the Estate of Antonio Machado; **Joan Margarit**: the author and Edicions Proa, Barcelona; **Hendrik Marsman**: Em. Querido Publishers, Amsterdam; **Caitlín Maude**: Cathal Ó Luain; **Xosé Luis Méndez Ferrín**: the author; **Miquel Martí i Pol**: from *Nova antologia poètica* (1997) © Grup 62, Barcelona; **José Moreno Villa**: José Moreno;

Giacomo Noventa: Marsilio Editori S.p.A., Venice; **Uxío Novoneyra**: Elva Rey and Via Lactea Editors (Merlin e Familia Collection);

Francesc Parcerisas: the author; **Chus Pato**: the author; **Octavio Paz**: Marie José Paz, from *El Girasol* (1943-1948), *Libertad bajo palabra*; **Sandro Penna**: Garzanti Libri (1997); **Emilio Prados**: © Herederos de Emilio Prados and Mercedes Casanovas Agency, Barcelona;

Pere Quart: Edicions Proa, Barcelona;

Nelo Risi: © Arnoldo Mondadori Editore S.p.A., Milan; **Bartomeu Rosselló-Porcèl**: 'Només un arbre' from *Imitació del foc* (1938), in *Obra Poètica de B. Rosselló-Porcèl* (Editorial Moll, Mallorca, 1998. Sixth edition);

Umberto Saba: © Arnoldo Mondadori Editore S.p.A., Milan; **Joan Salvat-Papasseit**: Editorial Ariel S.A., Barcelona; **Josep Sebastià Pons**: Àlex Susanna/Columna S.A.; **Àlex Susanna**: the author, Columna S.A., *Suite de Gelida* (2001) Edicions Proa, Barcelona.

Francesc Vallverdú: the author, from *Com Llances* (1961)/Óssa Menor, Barcelona.

Pearse Hutchinson and The Gallery Press thank Xosé Vizoso for permission to include his artwork in this book.

The publishers acknowledge also helpful advice from Alistair Carmichael/Carmichael Alonso libros, the Brazilian Embassy, Dublin, and Máire Ní Dhonnchadha/Irish Literature Exchange.

Every effort has been made to trace copyright holders of the work published in this book. Pearse Hutchinson and The Gallery Press apologise if any material has been included without permission or without the appropriate acknowledgement, and would be pleased to hear of any error or omission.